THE PERSONAL AURA

THE PERSONAL AURA

Dora van Gelder Kunz

*This publication made possible with
the assistance of the Kern Foundation*

QUEST BOOKS
The Theosophical Publishing House
Wheaton, Ill. U.S.A.
Madras, India/London, England

The Theosophical Publishing House
P.O. Box 270
Wheaton, IL 60189-0270

A publication of the Theosophical Publishing House,
a department of The Theosophical Society in America

Library of Congress Cataloging-in Publication Data

Kunz, Dora, 1904–
    The personal aura / Dora van Gelder Kunz.
       p. cm.
    ISBN 0-8356-0671-6 (pbk.) : $19.95
       0-8356-0675-6 (cloth) : $29.95
    1. Aura.   2. Aura—Case studies.   3. Theosophy.   I. Title.
BP573.A8K86 1991
133.8—dc20   90-50954
                                                       CIP

Printed in Singapore by Palace Press

To Emily Sellon
in appreciation of our long friendship
and of her arduous work editing this book

Contents

Foreword   — Renée Weber   ix

Chapter I   — The Background of the Book   1

Section I   —*The Structure and Dynamics of the Human Energy Fields*

Chapter II   — The Dimensions of Consciousness   11

Chapter III   — The Emotional Field   22

Chapter IV   — The Anatomy of the Aura   32

Section II   —*The Cycle of Life*

Chapter V   — The Development of the Individual   59

      1. A mother and unborn child   66
      2. A seven-months-old baby   72
      3. A four-year-old girl   77
      4. A seven-year-old boy   82
      5. An adolescent girl   85
      6. Maturity: an artist in her thirties   90
      7.   a man in his forties   94
      8. Old age: a woman in her nineties   99

Chapter VI   — The Dedicated Life   104

      9. A pianist/composer   105
      10. A concert pianist   110
      11. A social/environmental activist   114
      12. A painter   120
      13. A designer/architect   125
      14. A youthful idealist   129
      14a. Fifty-six years later   134

Chapter VII   — The Effects of Illness   138

      15. The results of polio   139
      16. A child born with Down's syndrome   144
      17. An acute anxiety state   147
      18. The effects of meditation upon a chronic heart patient   151

Contents

Section III   *— Possibilities for Change and Growth*

Chapter VIII — Healing and the Practice of Visualization   159

Chapter IX   — Changing Emotional Patterns   168

Chapter X   — Meditation and the Growth of Intuition   182

Foreword

Renée Weber, Ph.D.
Professor of Philosophy, Rutgers University

This book is a strangely ethereal and at the same time a completely practical, down-to-earth work, with vast philosophical implications. The ideas it presents can change our view of ourselves; they can enhance our understanding of our make-up, powers and influence, and hence of our responsibilities. Dora Kunz shows us to be linked in previously largely ignored ways to the universe and especially to other human beings, with whom we share influences that we do not suspect but that are spellbinding in their potential.

Dora Kunz's book describes human beings as immersed in energy-fields, akin to those described by physics but in many ways different: subtler, qualitatively charged, and knowable in terms of characteristics which — though not quantifiable by current scientific methods — are specific enough to be described. To a philosopher, the viewpoint of this book is of immense interest. It bears on many of the questions on which we have been speculating since the time of Pythagoras and Plato in ancient Greece, questions which basically are still unsettled. To me this work is of particular interest because, in addition, it agrees remarkably with a number of claims of Indian philosophy, my area of specialization. Many of the ideas which Dora Kunz presents in modern and often clinical form can be mapped directly on to Hindu and Buddhist accounts of metaphysics, physiology, psychology, and ethics.

Dora's book raises many challenging questions. The most crucial of these is the problem of how we — who cannot directly confirm or disconfirm her material — should regard her work. Although this is a difficult issue, certain basic remarks suggest themselves in weighing the status of her claims.

First, anyone familiar with Indian philosophy will recognize that the fields Dora describes are consistent with the teachings of both

Hindu and Buddhist thought. What we call field theory is central to Indian cosmology, metaphysics, ethics, and psychology — especially in yoga and meditation. Despite the important role which fields play in its theories, Indian philosophy fails to document these ideas adequately by Western criteria. Their existence is asserted and assumed, but without arguments to prove them. It is therefore philosophically important to find someone who approaches the subject empirically rather than theoretically.

The Indian thinkers to whom these subtle fields were self-evident discovered them through meditative and yogic practices. Patanjali, for example, describes them in medical and psychological as well as spiritual terms. But their modern clinical applications by Dora open new vistas of their practical value for human life in our time. This is true even if they are treated as no more than fruitful hypotheses whose effects can be tested in our lives.

In this brief Foreword, I can cite only a few concepts from Indian thought with which this book has similarities: the chakras; prana; subtle matter/energy systems; consciousness as the transformer of matter; the unity of all being; the idea of a universal field in which we are immersed (the Dharmakaya in Buddhism, Brahman in Hinduism); a spiritual universe without the need for a personal god; the validity of action-at-a-distance; the power of meditation; the role of space (or multidimensional space, *akasha*) in "registering" whatever happens in all dimensions, subtle or dense-material; a psychosomatic account of human functioning in both health and disease; the existence of clairvoyance and intuitive states of consciousness; karma (the law of universal causation); life after death and reincarnation.

Some of these concepts come up in specific ways in Dora's descriptions of the energy fields (or auras) and in their illustrated form in the paintings. Of the many questions they give rise to, probably the most troublesome one is the free-will/determinism question that has plagued philosophers and theologians for millennia. Are the potentialities and "karmic indicators" that Dora perceives in the infant and young child evidence of determinism, however loosely construed? How does our freedom to work out these "tendencies," (a freedom on which Dora insists) fit in with these "indicators"? Their presence entails our coming into the world with a certain character (or essence) and certainly not as the "blank tablets" that Locke, Skinner and contemporary behaviorists claim we are. These and other questions are philosophically crucial, and hence one looks with special interest at Dora's case histories, where some follow-up work of an individual's development over time is recorded.

Second, the energy fields Dora works with have an equally striking coherence with those described by science. Dora's observations fit the physicist David Bohm's theory of an Implicate Order, with its assertion that matter ranges from the dense, visible and physical through various states of decreasing density (in the Implicate Order) to states of such subtlety that they can no longer be thought of as "matter" at all but rather as mind or consciousness. Like Dora, Bohm asserts that subtle matter powerfully influences dense matter, and — although there is always some reciprocity — that the subtle has more power, because more wholeness, than the dense. It is in that sense an asymmetrical relationship, giving consciousness or thought a primary role in our health and well-being. Bohm and Dora both believe in a universal energy in which everything partakes; and, independently, they describe it in similar terms: for Bohm its qualities are intelligence and compassion, for Dora, order and compassion.

Dora's work and many of her assertions in this book also connect with physicist John Stewart Bell's theory of non-locality. This work is highly technical, but here is its essence: quantum mechanics reveals that every particle of matter in the universe is somehow in touch with and influences every other particle, even if they are separated by vast distances. David Bohm goes even further, for he claims that just as each particle is a record of all that happens in the universe, so do we at some level of our being possess that information. How close this picture comes to what Dora describes in her book I leave to the reader to decide.

Third, even though we know the physical fields of science only through their effects, as lay people we accept their existence because we trust the experts, namely the physicists. I emphasize this because I know of no way — except by analogy — to establish the reality or even the plausibility of these immensely subtle energy fields which are said powerfully to influence our lives.

For me, the idea of the human energy field must remain a hypothesis, however strong. For Dora it is a reality. She herself therefore becomes to a large extent the crucial factor in our assessment of her ideas. If one is interested in her work, one must — at least provisionally — trust her and her claim that these fields exist and that she is able to see and correctly interpret them.

Several analogies come to mind: skilled radiologists can read and correctly interpret what they see, hence explain what is happening within the body; the particle physicist and astrophysicist both work in an inferential way on data that also require interpretation. There are of course differences, for radiology and physics are in the public domain, where peers can evaluate one another's interpretations.

Public observation of auras is more difficult. The number of people said to perceive the human energy fields is minute; those able to interpret them medically and psychologically probably minuscule. In this domain, therefore, attention shifts unavoidably to the ability and reliability of the observer and interpreter. Who is this Dora Kunz, who has begun to map the territory of the human psyche in a new way? Since so much depends on her skill, clarity and integrity, it is essential to say something about her. I have known Dora for many decades, but despite our long and close friendship, she remains in many ways a mystery. I can provide a glimpse of her, but it is merely one perspective, filtered through my own experience.

Equally at ease with scientists, medical practioners and lay people, Dora is an unusual combination of traits. Her reputation as a clairvoyant often makes people conjure up an otherworldly being who practices her arcane art in a rarified atmosphere, but Dora does not fit these clichés. For one thing, she has a family life. Dora's forty-five year marriage to Fritz Kunz — a brilliant and intellectual man involved with mathematics, science, and philosophy — was exceptionally happy and lasted until his death in 1972. Her son, a Harvard graduate, is a computer consultant; her grandson, a Harvard mathematics graduate; her granddaughter, a recent graduate of Whitman College. Dora and her husband were devoted, sympathetic to one another's (very different) work, and completely supportive of each other's goals and activities. They were, each in a different way, powerful personalities.

Beyond these facts of Dora's normal (as opposed to her paranormal) life, she has had and continues to have a wide circle of friends from all walks of life. She is no prima donna, and does not hesitate to perform ordinary, practical tasks such as cooking for a crowd, organizing conferences and schedules, buying supplies, working in the garden, and so on. It would not occur to her to think of these as beneath her.

It is sometimes assumed that those gifted with paranormal powers lack normal ones. This, of course, is not true. Dora is intelligent, quick and incisive in her judgment, practical, and well-read. Everyone who knows her comments on her seemingly boundless energy. Her interests range from medicine and psychology to world affairs and national politics, and she communicates easily with a wide variety of people. I have seen strangers warm to her within minutes. This empathy doubtless is due to her ability to "tune in on" people and reach them at a level of consciousness different from the one at which they habitually function. This must account for the fact that an "interview" with Dora leaves one with a sense that deep aspects of oneself have been understood, both by her and by oneself. An acquaintance of mine — a successful and experienced psychiatrist who had already been through an analysis — once consulted Dora when he was at a crossroad in his life. "In all my life I have never felt so profoundly understood by anyone," he later told me. "I felt as if she could see right to the bottom of me. The nuances of her perception are without equal in my experience." A complex, skeptical and critical man, he offered the opinion that, although he did not believe in clairvoyance, he believed that Dora was indeed clairvoyant.

A second, even more important quality is Dora's unshakable integrity, which makes people trust and open up to her. Her life has been shaped by compassion for suffering, and she has placed her gifts for both "seeing" and counseling freely at the disposal of anyone who calls upon her, without accepting any rewards. She is, in short, an altruist.

To understand her at all and hence to understand this book, one must keep in mind that since childhood, Dora seems to have regarded her abilities as a trust. These of course are my words, not hers, for Dora's own attitude towards her gift is matter-of-fact and unsentimental. Nevertheless, one is struck by the fact that she never uses her clairvoyance in pursuit of the trivial, the frivolous, the sensational, for the sake of the curious, for personal gain, for power or control, or for any unethical reason. I dwell on this because her work entails such responsibility that the question of her motivation and integrity is critical.

Indispensable to a description of Dora's personality is mention of her independence of mind, strong will, and self-confidence, as well as her bluntness, impatience with details (except in her work), and keen sense of humor. These were probably encouraged and honed by her father, who early in her life seems to have schooled her in the Socratic method—the best proving ground I know of for developing a tough-minded attitude toward ideas.

For example, Dora is not a proselytizer or missionary for her ideas. If anything, she bends backwards. Her detached and casual attitude regarding people's view of her clairvoyance often results in a reticence that is irritating—if not maddening—to those who are genuinely interested in the kind of careful detail of which she is capable. I have seen a number of such encounters with individuals frustrated by Dora's (to me) unaccountable decision to hold back. Although she has become more open in the last two decades, she still seems less at ease in describing her work to lay people than to nurses, doctors, and other health professionals, i.e., those capable of testing or applying her findings in their work. This reticence may account for the long interval between her research and the publication of this book. Her decision to publish it is therefore all the more welcome. Since the data of the book were gathered through Dora's "interviews" with people, it may be appropriate here to state that these therapeutic sessions are one of her major altruistic contributions.

I know from my own experience as well as from the accounts of others that people come away from those interviews convinced that they can change. The anticipation of putting her various suggestions into practice, however at odds with one's past behavior these may be, fills one with optimism, a sense that "I can do this, I can change."

The anticipation of personal renewal mirrors Dora's deeply held belief that change is the law of life and that what we were last year matters less than what we make of ourselves today. This optimism may be one of her greatest gifts in working with people. During these interviews, one convincingly perceives the truth of what she says in her blunt and casual way, and one feels mobilized to act.

This book makes clear that within everyone lie the potential insight, strength, and will for real change. Dora devotes considerable time and energy to convincing others of the fact that hanging on to the past is harmful and to helping them find a way to let it go. This attitude is consistent with the great spiritual traditions, which teach that living in the present is the key to the spiritual life and even — notably in Buddhism — to a sane and fully awake life.

Lastly, the reader is challenged to test the reality of these energy fields in practice. Field theory has direct application to our personal and societal lives. The mere effort to test it in daily life makes one more sensitive to subtle realities, convincing one that indeed we are powerfully affected by the emotions and moods of others. This understanding can bring greater clarity and insight into our emotional lives.

As we enter the twenty-first century, we are living with two distinct models of man and nature, both relevant to this book. One is the materialistic, reductionistic model, which tries to account for nature and ourselves on the analogy of a machine. Humans, in this account, are like sophisticated supercomputers interacting with other supercomputers. This view continues to be dominant — particularly in philosophy but also in psychology. Side by side with it — and gaining increasing adherence — is the holistic and integrative model. This amounts to a philosophical revolution, a paradigm shift that forges a new picture of ourselves and our universe in its account of matter, energy, life, consciousness, and the human spirit. It envisions the interconnectedness of all beings and postulates the existence of as yet uncharted, powerful forces in nature and humanity which we can learn to draw on for changing our lives. The many strands in the holistic model are unified by a common assumption which provides them with a coherent and plausible philosophical framework.

In the holistic view, the universe is a living, dynamic, and orderly realm suffused with consciousness. It postulates the subtle states of matter already referred to, which are more properly the domain of psychology and consciousness. They deal with inward states that lie in dimensions not accessible to the ordinary mind. These — analogous to the multidimensional space of mathematicians and cosmologists — share a basic feature. All assert that certain aspects of reality cannot be understood within our old assumptions and classical frameworks.

Since the subtler dimensions of consciousness are inaccessible to the senses, they cannot be proven by physical means. However, the reality of multidimensional space is a postulate that underlies most of the concepts presented here, including meditation, healing, and the very real effect of our thoughts and feelings upon others. Even a conservative assessment must conclude that this new view of reality ranges from a fruitful working principle to a promissory note for the future. It is, in fact, an already-in-progress paradigm that encourages serious research. (A case in point is the status of therapeutic touch, an offspring of this worldview that is widely used by the nursing profession.)

The most novel feature of this hypothesis is the power it ascribes to human intentions. Nothing quite as diaphanous ("slippery!" its critics would proclaim) exists in contemporary science except the ambiguities and bewildering paradoxes of quantum mechanics. But if the new physics places the human observer at the center of the experimental situation, such subjectivity gains respectability and can surely be toler-ated in "the new psychology." And if the observer can affect the ob-served, by extension human consciousness can affect matter.

We are living in the midst of a scientific revolution whose philosophi-cal and spiritual meaning is far from clear. What is clear is that sweep-ing changes for our lives are in the making. Even at this early state, two inferences seem warranted: 1) twentieth century science and the faintly discernible outline of its future developments (in Bohm and Penrose, for example) are far more compatible with these ideas than was the science of earlier centuries; and 2) just as gravity, electromag-netism, and the strong and weak nuclear forces are the building blocks of physics, so are human intentionality and the power of the mind the building blocks for the work presented here. The assumption that our thoughts and feelings affect others forms the fundamental hypothe-sis of Dora's book.

These assumptions find no room within the mechanistic, Cartesian worldview in which we have been brought up and which we rarely question. The holistic view supplies the all-important missing element—the human factor. Applied, for example, to healing, car-ing, empathy, and compassion are subjective in that they originate with the practitioner, but objective in two ways: 1) they have conse-quences for both the self and the other; and 2) their power originates beyond the practitioner in the orderly processes of an infinite universe.

The sweeping assumptions I have been presenting imply a spiritual (though not necessarily a religious) dimension of reality. It is tempt-ing to conjecture that the fields Dora perceives may well constitute the elusive, long-sought bridge between physics and consciousness that turn up in the speculations of thinkers like Planck, Wheeler, Wigner, Wald, Bohm, Penrose, Bell, and others who seek to understand the philosophical and human meaning of their own work.

If we apply the connotations of "healing" and "healer" in their broad (rather than their restricted medical) context, we are all potential healers. This book shows us that sending peaceful energies to others is possible only if we ourselves are already in a peaceful state. We grow spiritually even as we try to help others. A corollary is that a negative attitude interferes with our ability to radiate harmonious energies. Emotions like anxiety, fear, jealousy, envy, resentment, anger, hatred, self-pity and the "victim-syndrome" that Dora refers to — in short, a down-beat outlook on ourselves, others, and the universe — will hinder our abilities to interact positively with others. Negativity, unfortunately, is widespread in our contemporary fragmented culture. It makes us feel helpless to affect events, small-scale or large. Dora's book counteracts this helplessness, for her point is that this need not be so.

She points the way to our becoming centers of caring, empathy, compassion, and harmony even amidst the chaos and suffering of our times. Dora encourages us to have confidence in our ability to change in positive ways which benefit us and others as well. To use meditation and project compassion for the good of others is neither narcissism nor escapism, criticisms sometimes leveled against spiritual practices. Marx's famous dismissal of religion as the "opiate of the people" does not fit the model of the healer, i.e., one who uses energies and intentions to help alleviate the pain and suffering in the world. Working to enhance the autonomy and self-confidence of others is not restricted to the medical model of healing. It is something constructive that all of us can do.

We can be a counter-force to the indifference, isolation, and abandonment of others that have become all too common in industrialized as well as underdeveloped societies. To radiate the power of compassion to a world torn by conflict and long-standing hatreds strikes me as an unassailable ideal. Thus, the ethical implications of this remarkable book can scarcely be overstated.

I
The Background of the Book

The series of aura portraits which are a central feature of this book came into being in a spontaneous, unpremeditated way, the result of circumstances rather than any intention or plan on my part.

I had for some time been working with my friend, Dr. Otelia Bengtsson, a medical doctor who was in private practice in New York City in the field of allergy and immunology. Since problems of this kind frequently have psychosomatic aspects, she had thought that my clairvoyance might be helpful in some of her cases which were difficult to diagnose or resistant to treatment. Since she is one of the most selfless and courageous doctors I have ever known, she had no qualms about bringing patients to see me, although at that time (the early 1930's) such unorthodox behavior in a physician was much more unusual than it would be today.

As a rule I knew nothing about the cases, although I was of course aware of Dr. Bengtsson's specialty and always saw the patients in her presence. I would tell her what I thought the physical problems were, but I also explained the role that the patients' emotions played in the disease process, and gave advice about the ways in which they could help themselves.

Even during adolescence I had been asked to help people who were in pain or disturbed, and in that way I had learned to observe emotional patterns and to interpret what I saw. But my work with Dr. Bengtsson taught me to be a careful observer, and gave me the opportunity to study in depth the relationships between emotional patterns and physical disease—a work that I have continued to practice over the years. Her confidence in me was tremendously helpful, since without her cooperation I would not have had the possibility of long-term study of the disease process and its psychological correlates. Since the time that the pictures in this book were made, I have seen hundreds, even thousands, of people who have come to me for help, and I find these contacts a continuing learning experience.

The paintings came about because many years ago I had made friends with a gifted artist, Juanita Donahoo, who was very much interested in my descriptions of auras and wanted to try her hand at illustrating them. She had begun to experiment with the air brush, and thought that it might be a good medium to use in trying to convey some idea of the misty, blended and ever-changing hues of the aura. She was interested and eager, and very willing to experiment in various ways in order to adapt her medium to what I saw.

I must say that it was a very tedious process. Juanita had an elaborate color chart, and as I described the person who was sitting before us she would make a rough drawing of the aura, putting in the special features, plotting the areas of color and matching these as closely as possible to what I said I saw. I am afraid I was not always easy to satisfy, because the colors of pigment, no matter how subtle, are infinitely coarser and duller than those of the astral world. She was patience itself. But even so, I have to say that these pictures are only a faint approximation of the reality, although Juanita's efforts would be difficult to better, for she was very sensitive and receptive to the impressions I was trying to convey.

These aura paintings represent a series of portraits of people with whom I had some contact, or who were brought to me by others, and show them as they were (or as I perceived them to be) at that point in time. This is a fact I want to emphasize. These are portraits of individuals—some famous, some obscure, some older, some younger—not, of course, of their faces or figures, but of their personalities and character as they were at that moment in their lives. It is a record of their interests, work, feelings, aspirations, talents and potentialities, as well as their problems, difficulties and emotional habits.

Each person would come prepared to sit for us for two to three hours, and some of them found it rather boring. I especially remember one well-known musician who became very restless before we were even half-way through the session. Fortunately his daughter had brought a musical score with her, and after she handed this to him he became so engrossed in it that he was unconscious of the passage of time.

Other subjects were intrigued by having their auras sketched, and wanted to know what the different colors meant. One man especially responded to this information in a characteristic way. When told that the orange plume in his aura was a sign of pride and self-assurance, he said, "I don't like that and I'm determined to change it." As for the children, they ran about or played with toys or even took short naps. These activities did not disturb us in the least, since it was quite normal behavior and showed that they were relaxed.

Thus the paintings are portraits of individuals, not generalizations or composite pictures such as those that illustrate other books on the aura, like C. W. Leadbeater's *Man Visible and Invisible*. These are real people, with great personality differences. I shall talk about the nature of the aura in subsequent chapters, but I want to emphasize at the outset that these portraits are like a still frame in a moving picture — a glimpse caught in the midst of the on-going process of living. We all have changing moods, and these are reflected in the aura, overlaying the more permanent features. Therefore the aura pictures capture the essence of these individuals in terms of what they were feeling at that point in time.

Subjects of the Study

There is something else I must emphasize. These portraits do not represent a cross-section of society — perhaps not even a fairly typical group of people, although we have a range of ages. There is an even balance between females and males, but this is a matter of chance, not design. There are no murderers, no criminals, no psychotics. Most of these people are from the middle class; none are examples of greed, lust, anger, cruelty, violence or other compulsive behavior. Some are quite ordinary, but a few are unusually gifted, and a considerable proportion has philosophical, humanitarian and spiritual interests. Thus we lack the contrast which would have been afforded by the inclusion of some anti-social personalities.

The reason for this lack of variety is that we never thought of the enterprise as a clinical psychological inquiry. It was a study of the aura, pure and simple. At that time, a number of people had expressed interest in my clairvoyant observations, which seemed more detailed than others then available. They wanted to see what an aura looked like, and how personality differences showed themselves. So we began and ended with the people who were immediately accessible and willing to sit for us. We did not try to get a mix of people with different ethnic, cultural, religious or educational backgrounds.

If I were to undertake such a project today I should do it very differently. These studies were made about fifty-five years ago, when I was still quite young, and although my clairvoyant faculties have not changed, I have since learned a great deal more about human interactions. In this book, the aura pictures and descriptions are the product of my early observations, but I have tried to give them additional substance in the other chapters, which are more representative of what I have learned in the intervening years.

Some readers may also wonder why we have waited such a long time before publication. One of the reasons is contained in what I have just said: I did not feel ready to undertake a general study of the personal aura based on these few examples. The second, more important reason is that the intellectual climate in those days would not have been conducive to any serious consideration of the concepts which are essential to the subject.

It is only during the past few decades that advances in science, in medicine and in psychology have brought about a changing perception of the role of consciousness in human life. Now there is much more acceptance of the mind-body relationship and the psychosomatic origins of disease, as well as a recognition of the importance of attitudes in human interactions. As a result, there is today a context within which what I have to say may not seem so strange.

Recently, in working through the paintings, we began to see that they fall into certain patterns or groupings, and that these reveal characteristics which have little to do with the fame or obscurity of the person. Most individuals have certain basic emotional characteristics in common: love and sympathy, intellectual capacity — the ability to learn, to express themselves and to accomplish some meaningful work. Readers will, I hope, find it interesting to trace these innate human abilities in terms of the quite different kinds of people represented in the pictures, and perhaps recognize themselves therein to some degree.

Finally, the reader may wish to know something of my background, which makes it possible for me to perceive the aura or (as I like to call it) the emotional field of a person.

Personal History

I was born into a Dutch family living on a large plantation in Java, where my father was the manager of a sugar factory. Both my mother and my grandmother had psychic abilities, but in no way could these be called inherited. If genetic factors are involved, they probably relate to an innate sensitivity, and to the ability to respond intuitively to unforeseen situations and events. At birth I was completely enveloped in a caul (the foetal membrane), which is supposed to signify second sight, and I am told that I broke this with my fist, and so liberated myself.

My mother was a strong believer in meditation, and always set aside a room which was never used for any other purpose. She started me in the practice when I was about five years of age. At first she suggested very simple themes to me, but later she asked me to meditate upon abstract questions, and she and my father would expect me to give them an account of the ideas which had come to me as a result.

As for my clairvoyance, I suppose I began to become aware of it and to develop it when I was around six or seven years of age. At about that time, C. W. Leadbeater (who was a famous clairvoyant and theosophical writer) came to visit us, and he was very much interested in me and what I saw. Later on, when I was about twelve years old, we went to live in Australia and I was in contact with him daily for a number of years. I cannot say that he ever trained me in the use of my clairvoyance, but he did put specific tasks to me — some of which were very difficult for a shy young girl — and through trying to accomplish these tasks I learned to have more confidence in myself.

But perhaps the early training which has been most useful to me came from my father's insistence that I think for myself and learn to uphold my ideas in spite of opposition. My father loved argument, and he made me defend the positions I took, so that I learned I could not take anything for granted.

Thus at an early age I was taught not to expect that people would necessarily agree with me. This has stood me in good stead in my work with the medical profession, for if I happen to be associated with doctors who are skeptical about my clairvoyance, this attitude does not seem unreasonable to me and never interferes with my willingness to collaborate with them. In other words, I am not bothered by the fact that people may think clairvoyance is nonsense, for I believe that every person has the right to accept the claims of others only if they make sense to him or her.

I offer the following descriptions and discussions of the emotional field from this point of view. To me, emotional patterns result from many factors and different life experiences, some good, some painful, some negative, some constructive. If we are not aware of these patterns they can inhibit us in many ways and even lead to the beginnings of the disease process. However, emotions are not only volatile but also charged with energy, and therefore they can and do change.

What is more, the direction which that change takes is subject to our own intention, once that becomes clear to us.

My hope in writing this book is that it may help readers see their own emotional patterns more clearly, and thus understand the possibilities for change and growth that lie within all of us.

I
The Structure and Dynamics of the Human Energy Fields

II
Dimensions of Consciousness

The life of even the most ordinary person, which may seem very un-eventful, is actually full of experiences on many levels. While we are focused on the daily business of living, we are at the same time involved in a whole complex of interactions between physical processes, feelings and thoughts. Though we may not pay much attention to these interactions, they constantly influence our behavior, as well as our sense of well-being.

What I try to do in this book is share with you something of my perception and appreciation of the hidden dimensions of consciousness within us, and in so doing, make you more aware of these aspects of your own life, and of your ability to effect conscious changes in yourself.

My focus is principally upon our feelings, for the aura — the luminous cloud of color surrounding each of us — is the personal emotional field. But our feelings are part of the larger whole we call a human being, and therefore they are inseparable from everything else that goes on within us. The interactions between mind, emotions and physical energies are so rapid and so constant that they blur these differentiations, and so we usually only notice them when they break down. Therefore, in order to understand the nature of the emotions and the role they play, we have to see them from the perspective of the whole person — and this includes not only the body, mind and feelings, but also still higher dimensions of consciousness.

Higher Dimensions of Consciousness

Theosophical, Indian and other literature has identified the nature of these higher states, and given them various names. While I always recommend that people study this literature for themselves and make their own judgments, for present purposes I will simply offer my own descriptions and use my own terms, which I hope to make as simple and clear as possible.

For many reasons, I prefer to think of the different states of consciousness not as "planes," as they have been called in earlier descriptions, but as dimensions, or fields. Both these words suggest the possibility of movement within an open, dynamic space, and also of an almost infinite expansion into higher reaches of consciousness. Both imply the existence of a greater whole of which the various dimensions or fields are aspects, and within which they constantly interact. In speaking about the human energy fields, I always try to emphasize that everything—including ourselves—exists in terms of this greater whole, which is the universe itself. All the dimensions of consciousness are present everywhere, in everything, even if only in a rudimentary state.

Consciousness

Consciousness takes many forms, and its ranges extend far beyond what we ordinarily think of as the conscious mind. The various states go all the way from primitive body awareness at one extreme to the highest reaches of spiritual insight at the other. Thus they form a hierarchical system, in that the energies associated with the various states of consciousness become increasingly refined as they move into the higher dimensions. But this does not mean that any one of these states is negligible, or less important than the rest. If we try to see all of the dimensions in terms of the whole of which they are a part, we see that each one has a unique part to play within the total spectrum of consciousness.

Lama Govinda has explained this very well: "The consciousness of a higher dimension consists in the coordinated and simultaneous perception of several systems of relationship or directions of movement in a wider, more comprehensive unity, without destroying the individual characteristics of the integrated lower dimensions. The reality of a lower dimension is therefore not annihilated by a higher one, but only . . . put into another perspective of values."[1]

In the same sense, when I speak of "higher dimensions" or "higher levels" I am not trying to make value judgments, but merely describing the "systems of relationship" which Lama mentions above. Indeed, value judgments are inappropriate when we are trying to understand the nature of the different dimensions of consciousness. It is more to the point to study their functions and characteristics, and become aware of their special contributions — as well as their limitations — in terms of that far greater reality which is the whole of human nature.

Looked at in this way, states of consciousness are actual conditions which are *different* from one another but not *separate* — either from each other or from the body itself. The subtle fields co-exist within the same space, and influence each other. Their distinctiveness lies in the fact that each has its own unique type of energy and rate of vibration. This makes it possible for the various fields to exert their special effects and at the same time interpenetrate and interact with the other fields without interference.

It is difficult to find an exact analogy to this phenomenon in terms of ordinary experience. Perhaps the whole effect is achieved in somewhat the same way that the unique sound of a musical chord is created by combining different tones, each of which can be distinguished by a trained ear. The experience of listening to music is the best analogy I can think of, because the differences between the subtle fields are essentially *harmonic* in nature. Each dimension of consciousness has its range of frequencies, and plays a particular part in the total orchestration of a human being.

---

1. Lama Anagarika Govinda, *Foundations of Tibetan Mysticism*, E.P. Dutton, N.Y. 1960, p.218.

Radiant Energies

Not being a scientist, I can only suggest how it may be possible to perceive the subtle fields. We know that sound and light are forms of radiant energy which have different wavelengths, and that many phenomena beyond our sense perception, such as ultraviolet light, become accessible to us only when we have the instruments to detect them. To me, the higher dimensions are forms of radiant energy related to light. Just as sunlight can be broken up into the spectrum we see as a rainbow, so these higher energies reveal themselves through their characteristic colors. It is these that I perceive. Therefore, clairvoyance may be an instrument which makes some otherwise invisible wavelengths and frequencies come within the range of perception.

When questions about clairvoyance arise, one of the greatest stumbling blocks for most people lies in the fact that the ability to see subtler dimensions seems to be limited to a few people. While I am unable to account for this, I want to point out that until modern times it was impossible to see viruses, or distinguish ultrasonic waves, or examine genetic material. All these things existed before there were instruments which made it possible to observe them, and it may well be that in the future the mechanism of clairvoyance will be investigated and understood. As of now, I can only say that I achieve my clairvoyance by a shift of visual focus. It is under my control, and I use it only when I choose to do so. I use the word "visual" to describe the process because it is a kind of seeing, but the actual eyes are not involved. It is more a focusing of attention. I use my clairvoyance primarily in my work, and my ordinary vision is just like that of anybody else.

To me, vitality, feeling and thinking are forms of energy. Although most of us do not think of them in this way, a number of scientists whom I have consulted say it is legitimate to use the word "energy" in connection with the emotions, since energy means "the capacity of acting or producing an effect." We accept physical fields like gravitation as "real," because although we never see them we experience their effects directly. At the moment, due to our lack of more information, the nature of the subtle fields can only be assumed from the ways in which they affect us. I always try to emphasize that feelings are not just subjective psychological states; they have real physical consequences, and influence our health in many ways. I speak from personal experience, for this is an area in which I have been observing and working all my life.

The Spectrum of Consciousness

Regarded as energies, feelings and thoughts are related to one another in a way that is analogous to the relationship between sound and light. At one end of the spectrum of consciousness lies the field most closely related to the physical body. It is known as the etheric, and its characteristic form of energy is what is called *prana* in Indian thought — that is, life energy or vitality. All living things are nourished and sustained by this energy. In diagnosing illness, the color and radiance of an individual's pranic flow are important indicators to me of the state of health. The reason why the emotions have such an impact upon our health is because the etheric is very closely linked with the emotional field; there is a constant interplay between the two types of energy.

Incidentally, this is the most difficult field to study clairvoyantly, because it is the most complex. The etheric is really the prototype of the physical body, and it replicates the complexities of our bodily processes. In looking for traces of disease, therefore, one must take note of variations in color, texture, degree and type of motion, and many other factors within the etheric. In the practice of healing techniques such as Therapeutic Touch, we work primarily to discover and remove impediments in the flow of etheric energy, while always thinking of the person as a whole. A discussion of the etheric and its functions is not appropriate here, but those readers who would like a fuller description might be interested in a book which I wrote with Dr. Shafica Karagulla, called *The Chakras and the Human Energy Fields.*[2]

---

2. Shafica Karagulla and Dora Kunz, Theosophical Publishing House, *The Chakras and the Human Energy Fields*, Wheaton, Ill. 1989.

Next in order of subtlety of material and speed of motion comes the astral or emotional field, whose characteristic form of energy is feeling, followed by the mental, whose energy is thought or thinking. Beyond lie the intuitional field and still subtler levels. These dimensions are increasingly finer in texture, lighter, faster moving, and have higher rates of vibration. They are more powerful, because they are able to transform coarser energies into finer. They are more open to spiritual influences, and they are also more enduring, since they are less affected by the storms and stresses of physical life.

As I mentioned, our tendency is to think of things that are "higher" as being "better," but this is not necessarily the case with the relationship between mind and feeling. On the level of daily activity, these two faculties ordinarily work closely together. As soon as we feel something we rationalize that feeling, and place it in the context of our experience, so that our emotions and thoughts are constantly interacting.

The Mind

The mind can influence the emotions very powerfully, because it is that part of us which can distance itself from our feelings and observe their effects: "I feel happy; I feel angry." Thus the mind can give more objectivity to our emotions by pointing out the direction in which they are leading us, and by so doing, produce order and coherence in our lives. But the mind can also become warped and exert an egotistic, negative and harmful effect upon the emotional life. It can justify our prejudices and pervert the truth, thus becoming, as H. P. Blavatsky put it, "the slayer of the real."

Yet the mind's influence is essential for personal integration and balance, as well as for guidance. It is the mind that sets goals, plans strategies, formulates problems and works them out step by step. Reason offers guidance, gives shape and coherence to our wandering thoughts, permits self-criticism. All these are the positive uses of the mind in daily life.

There is also a level of the mind which is engaged with abstract thinking, such as mathematics, philosophy or science, and this does not affect the emotions directly to the same extent. However, mathematicians and scientists would not pursue their profession unless it aroused their interest, which is needed to engage emotional drive, focus attention and kindle enthusiasm for an abstract enterprise. Some people have a real passion for ideas and can become totally absorbed in them; such interest is far from being merely academic. In this case, emotional and mental energies are working fully together, which is one of the signs of personal integration.

But there is all too often a gap, a lack of synchronism, between the reason which tries to understand a situation and the feelings which make us act. Often people do not heed the information so offered, but directly act out what their feelings dictate at the moment. Then our emotional drives can lead us into behavior which does not accord with our intention, or even with our experience. In such a case we say that a person is impulsive — even, perhaps, to the extent of being out of control. Such splits in the psyche show up visibly in the personal aura of an individual. The mental field can be open to the intuition as well as being clear and well focused, but the individual may not be well-balanced at the emotional level. When this happens, there may be a fertility of ideas without the ability to follow through and put them into practice.

There are many such kinds of dysfunction between the fields. However, except in the very ill or disabled, the emotional and mental fields always work together quite closely, for thinking is as a matter of course accompanied by some degree of feeling. It may be interest or boredom, like, dislike or indifference, but even when repressed, there is always an emotional component in our thought.

The Intuition

Our feelings for nature or for beauty or for world peace are also emotions, but of a different kind. They go beyond the purely personal, and are linked with that aspect of ourselves which we call the intuition. This is a level of consciousness which is beyond the mind, or lies deeper within us, and it gives us insights which reach beyond our knowledge. Many people have had a sudden experience of unity with nature — or with the spiritual component of the world — so strongly that for the moment it dissolved all the barriers that separate us from one another. Such a unitive experience transcends both mind and emotion, suffusing them with higher-level energies so powerful that the result can be an entirely new perspective on life.

In a different case, insight — seeing the whole of a relationship or the truth of an idea — is also an aspect of the intuitive field, for it is both more sudden and more direct than our usual cause-and-effect thinking. It is this that makes it possible for us to see new truths in old situations, to find creative solutions to intractable problems and to make sudden, quantum jumps in understanding.

The Experience of Time

There is another point to note about the subtle fields that seems to indicate that they really are dimensions of space. The experience of time is different in these higher dimensions. I do not understand how or why this should be so, except that we all know that time is relative to motion. Since the dynamics of the subtler fields are different from those of the physical world, time values on these levels are much more flexible. Past and present, as we know them, lose much of their distinctiveness and become part of one time continuum. Both are represented to some extent in the here and now of the emotional and mental fields. This is why it is possible to discover traces of the distant past in a person's aura, and to forecast tendencies which may develop in the future. The way this time factor becomes part of the individual human psyche will be touched upon in describing the auras of babies and children.

Although we may be unaware of the different states of consciousness and energy within us, we make use of them as easily as the air we breathe, for they are part of the natural world. But what makes it possible for us to draw upon all these energies without being conscious of them? What is the principle of integration which coordinates and unifies all the physical, vital, emotional and mental dimensions within us?

The Timeless Self

I believe that this integrating factor is what I like to call the "timeless self" — a principle of being which provides continuity during life, and persists after death. This is a concept which occurs mainly in Hinduism (where it is linked to reincarnation), although it is kin to the soul as described in Christianity. However it be defined, from my point of view that self is a reflection of the ultimate aspect of being. It is rooted in a timeless spiritual reality which transcends and embraces all the dimensions of consciousness.

As will be shown in the aura pictures, especially those of children, everyone is born with a link to this spiritual reality, whether or not this link is ever consciously realized during life. The self (which should not be confused with the ego or egotism) is the thread which not only connects us to reality, but also gives ultimate shape, meaning and value to our experience. It is the power of the timeless self within us that makes it possible for human beings to overcome the greatest obstacles. Even severely handicapped people can draw upon this inner strength. By so doing, they can develop their own creativity and find it possible to make a contribution — not physically, perhaps, but on the level of human relations.

I have a dear friend who illustrates this point in a remarkable way. As an infant she contracted polio, which left her extremely disabled. She is confined to a wheelchair, has lost the use of her left arm, and is neurologically impaired in a variety of ways. In spite of all this, she has never been without the confidence that she would be able to function in the world.

Although her health is always precarious, her courage and her creative potential have made it possible for her to overcome many of the obstacles to a full life. She was able to study painting and develop her artistic gifts to the extent that she has been capable of earning her own living, at least partially. Although she is in constant pain, she never complains and is always interested in the lives of other people. As a consequence, she has dozens of friends. The realization that she is able to make a contribution to others in spite of all her difficulties has sustained her spirit throughout her life.

This story illustrates a point I shall be emphasizing in different ways throughout this book. With determination, and the self-confidence it inspires, we can draw upon an almost limitless potential of higher energies within us, giving us the ability to achieve goals which might seem far beyond our capacities.

The Effects of Karma

Lastly, there is the question of personal idiosyncrasy. We are all born with a basic emotional pattern, or with the possibility of developing certain emotional qualities, as I shall try to show in discussing the auras of children. In this connection, it is impossible to ignore the question of karma (the effects of past action), which sets the boundary conditions of human life. These conditions are not cast in concrete, because karma can work itself out in many ways and on many different levels. Nevertheless, it establishes certain predispositions which a person will have to cope with during life, and these are clearly represented at the level of the emotions.

Today we have become used to the idea that we are born with certain genetic patterns that determine our physical make-up and also govern our mental processes and emotional responses. This is true to a certain extent, but our knowledge of the genes does not yet encompass the ways in which mental and emotional characteristics are formed, or how they will develop. Medicine is finding ways to change genetic patterns and perhaps eliminate hereditary defects, but will such changes make people more humane, kinder, more compassionate? Most of us accept the fact that illness affects our mental and emotional states, but not that the reverse is also true.

Human beings have far greater depths within them than one might suppose. As I remarked at the beginning of this chapter, the subtle dimensions of consciousness are in many ways more powerful than our physical attributes.

We all have access to these inner resources. They are not reserved for the few, the privileged or the especially gifted, for they are part of our human heritage. Even when they remain an untapped resource, they are there, always available if we have the will and the motivation to use them.

III
The Emotional Field

No human being is without feelings. From a baby's first cry to a dying person's last look at friends and family, our primary response to the world around us is colored by emotion. Whether that world seems to us friendly or frightening, beautiful or ugly, pleasant or disagreeable affects the way we approach others, and indeed influences everything we do. I do not believe that such feelings arise in us solely due to environmental conditions, or to genetic factors, however important these both may be. Members of the same family, placed in the same kinds of situations, react in very different ways. Our emotions are a conscious response to our experience, but they are self-generated and reveal something important about our character.

To me, the emotions are "real" in the sense that I can perceive them objectively as a luminous atmosphere surrounding every living being. Because of its luminosity, this material has traditionally been called "astral" — i.e., "shining" — in theosophical literature.

Every time we feel an emotion there is a discharge of energy in the emotional field, whether slight or strong, and this produces a characteristic vibration and a color — the "footprint" of that particular emotion.

From experience I have learned to identify the principal shades and tones of color which the emotions produce, although the subtle variations are almost infinite. Since we are continually feeling a succession of different emotions during daily life, these colors are sometimes fleeting, passing like tinted clouds through the aura — our personal field or atmosphere—or suffusing it with a sudden tide of strong color. Other emotions are much more enduring, and these become a more or less permanent feature of the aura.

In the previous chapter, I spoke of the fact that it is often difficult for people to accept feelings as a form of energy which can be observed and even measured. To restate the claim, if emotions do have definite effects in terms of our physical and psychological health, they must possess some kind of force, or energy. And since in our universe energy is always associated with matter, the emotions must be in some sense material or related to material phenomena. Even if the matter of the emotional field is finer and more tenuous than any that has so far been studied by science, this does not mean it is "supernatural" (which is a word I dislike intensely). The emotional field—like the physical world with all its subtleties—is part of the structure of the universe itself, both visible and invisible, and is, I believe, subject to the same natural laws.

Thus although the emotional field is not yet accessible to physical observation, it is in some sense "material." Lama Govinda spoke about the "individual characteristics" of the lower dimensions of consciousness. It is the special characteristics of the emotional field that I shall be talking about, because in considering the personal aura we must never forget that it is part of the much larger field which is the aura of the Earth itself. We are never separated from this larger whole.

The emotional field appears to consist of a translucent, semi-transparent medium. It is unique in that the light which shines through it is broken up into a thousand different hues, but the source of that light does not come from without; it is generated by the medium itself. The emotional field is self-luminous.

The fabric of the emotional field is also permeable, in that it is interpenetrated by physical as well as subtler fields. However, as I have said, because of their different rates of vibration the fields do not blend or merge, but maintain their own integrity. Surrounding every person there is an etheric "body" which interpenetrates the physical body and extends outwards some three to five inches. The aura, or emotional field, interpenetrates the etheric, but extends much farther into space. The mental and intuitional fields similarly interpenetrate and extend beyond the emotional. Thus the personal fields assume the appearance of concentric spheres. Yet at the same time each of these personal fields is part of a universal field that contains everything and is associated with the Earth itself.

Emotions and mental images, therefore, can be thought of as refined states of matter with their corresponding types of energy. I happen to be able to perceive these. But at the non-physical levels it is not just a question of being able to see colors and patterns; perception is very closely related to another faculty, which could be called empathy. It is this that permits observers to understand what they are looking at. Observation simultaneously involves the act of seeing and rapport with what is seen. Without this faculty of empathy, the shapes and colors would have very little meaning. As a matter of fact, the ability to perceive astral colors is not uncommon, but unfortunately the ability to interpret their meanings has not been widely developed.

The emotions are closely linked with the physical body during life, but the astral field is not restricted to the living. A discussion of after-death states is not the subject of this book, but if one is to understand the nature of the emotions and of the astral field in general, it is necessary to think of them as a particular state of consciousness — not just an attribute of physical life or of brain function. They are an essential expression of the self. In the previous chapter I mentioned that I think of the self as the point or principle of integration within a human being. It is around such a point that mental and emotional configurations center, and thereby become meaningful to us and useful in our experience.

The Self as a Principle of Integration

Looked at in this way, it is possible to think of the self as transcending the physical body and as more enduring than our emotional and mental states, which we all know change from time to time. This concept of the self, or selfhood, as an integrating principle has been used by some scientists to identify the point of departure in every learning process — that is, where, not when, learning begins. Erich Jantsch even suggests that self-organization is a property of the universe itself, and that "Evolution, at least in the domain of the living, is essentially a learning process."[1] We could ask, who or what is it that learns — in the sense of absorbing and then applying the fruits of experience? I certainly cannot accept that it is merely a mechanical function of the brain, for to me every mountain, river, tree, plant and animal has a degree of consciousness and of personality, or "selfhood." This is why we feel an affinity for certain places; they have their own unique character that draws us to them.

Our usual linear sense of time, which is so important in daily life, does not dominate this learning process. On the one hand the assimilation of experience is on-going — it never stops — and on the other, learning is an experience in depth, related to the nature of the self. Memories, associations, insights, ideals, aspirations, creative ideas, unselfish love — all persist long after the fact, gradually distilling their essence into the depths of our consciousness. Thus they become an ineradicable element of our nature, and contribute to our personal growth and evolution.

The Astral World

Like the earth's atmosphere, the emotional field is ever-present, and it plays an essential role during life. It can quite legitimately be called the astral "world," because it replicates, in its own way, the features of the physical world. So far as I know, there is an emotional counterpart of everything in the physical world (people, animals, plants, rocks, even molecules). There is an astral landscape, as it were. Since feelings are not so stable as physical things, this landscape has some of the characteristics of a dream world. But there are degrees of sta-

---

1. *The Self-Organizing Universe*, Erich Jantsch, Pergamon Press, 1980, p.7.

ceptibly change the emotional field as a whole. Yet if we reflect on our own interpersonal relations — not only in the family, but in social and professional life as well — we see how this influence can grow. Our response to people we instinctively like, as well as those we don't, often results from our interaction at the emotional level. The aura of every person is a composite of emotional characteristics to which our own feelings resonate. Of course we are often mistaken in such quick judgments, because emotional responses are based more upon compatibility than on character, but the strength of the interaction is real.

Since the emotional field is an open system, it is always capable, in varying degrees, of interacting with the fields of those around us. I say in varying degrees, because some of us are more sensitive than others. Such sensitives take in some of the emotional energy which another person is feeling, so there can be an emotional exchange without a word having been spoken. However, some people feel another's emotion without being able to interpret it clearly, and therefore may misunderstand its cause. For example, we may be in contact with a person who is disturbed for some reason which has nothing to do with us, and yet we may feel the effects of the disturbance. People are frequently hurt or angered by this sort of misinterpretation. If this becomes a persistent condition it may result in a fear of interacting with others.

Interpersonal Relationships

This observation applies as well to family and other close relationships, and in fact to all human interactions. In many ways, human relationships can be the most painful experiences in our lives, or the most helpful and rewarding. But we are on the whole not aware of the degree to which our emotional reactions affect those close to us. All interpersonal relationships are vulnerable to violent emotional interchanges, a fact which people do not seem to realize until the damage is done. None of us can completely escape the effects of our mental and emotional environments, even though we do not consciously recognize what is happening. We can be stimulated or saddened, made peaceful or uneasy, by the places and situations we find ourselves in. This is particularly true for children, who are often more sensitive than adults to the emotional atmosphere.

Today, in a world characterized by so many broken homes, children very often feel that they are alone except for their relationships with other children, because there is no basis for emotional trust between the parents. When children are left alone to go their own way, they can easily take to drugs. Children need consistent relationships and an atmosphere of security, and if they do not find these at home they will seek them among other children in the street.

The state of our emotional environment can be quite unrelated to the degree of comfort and beauty — or the lack of these — within our physical circumstances. Beyond this, there is the larger environment created by the attitudes and feelings of our culture, both national and international. It is fairly easy for people to imagine the personal aura, and the pictures which illustrate this book may help in this regard. But it is more difficult to think of space itself as charged with emotional energies. Nevertheless this idea is important, because it helps us to understand how the energies of the whole field constantly impact us. And this is not just a one-way process. The field affects us, and we affect the field, even if in different degree. All of us contribute our thoughts and feelings to what can be called the emotional component of the world, and this contribution is not negligible. It is, in fact, a force for evolutionary change in terms of human growth and development.

Resonance

I have said that the interactions between fields are based on a principle of resonance which I do not understand, even though I observe its results. In the case of the emotions, anyone who has a tendency towards a particular kind of emotional energy will resonate to its presence. For example, when a person is aroused to a powerful emotion such as rage, this energy is discharged into the emotional field, where it amplifies the anger that is already there. As a result, anyone else who is easily aroused to anger could have the tendency aggravated; the feeling would be amplified like a standing wave.

Wars, natural disasters and even events like a stock market crash produce widespread anxiety, and this runs like wildfire around the world, infecting more and more people, who in turn amplify the contagion. When people are swept by sudden fear or anger they become more vulnerable to such intensifications of the emotional field, and then emotional storms can cause panics or waves of violence. We have all seen pictures of crowds gone wild under the influence of such mass emotion.

But we do not need to let ourselves be engulfed by the contagion of negative emotions. It is possible to remain calm even when we are surrounded by violence, and this steadiness can attenuate the anger and dissipate it. Even when we are in the presence of anger, we do not need to let it resonate within us. The antidote lies in positive feelings such as peace, compassion and sympathy, for these are more powerful than the negative emotions and strengthen us to reject them.

Nature's Healing Energies

This is why people feel refreshed when they leave the city — stimulating though it may be — for the peace of the country. Nature has a powerful influence upon us because it is charged with energies which can affect us directly. In this period of history, when the pressures of life are exacerbated more each day, and people are densely crowded together, there is all the more need to achieve some quiet within ourselves. Nature can and does provide a sense of harmony and peace, because even though it may be subjected to the turbulence of wind and storm, it is totally without emotional conflict.

In nature the spiritual elements which sustain life are always present. Thus, being in touch with the land or the mountains or the sea can enhance our ability to meet our personal storms — and even the hostility and violence of others — with strength and steadiness. When we are able to do this, we refuse to succumb to negative feelings, even when they are thrown at us. What is more, we are making a contribution to world peace, because we are influencing and modifying the emotional field as a whole, instead of merely reacting to it.

Today more and more people are becoming environmental activists, trying to help heal the wounds which human ignorance and greed have inflicted upon our Earth. Such attitudes can have a dramatic effect in reversing the exploitation which nature has suffered at our hands. The next step in the process of rehabilitation is for human beings to realize that their own attitudes, thoughts and feelings can have an equal effect upon the level of tension and violence in the world. We can influence the emotional atmosphere we all share in positive ways, and thus make a contribution to the well-being of everyone.

IV
The Anatomy of the Aura

A great deal has been written about the aura and the astral world in general. While it might be useful for the reader to have some acquaintance with this literature, I want to emphasize that the descriptions and information that appear in this book are the result of my own experience and investigations, and are not derived from other sources. Therefore they may disagree in some particulars with other accounts. This is not because those accounts are necessarily incorrect (or that my own are), but because in all observation so much of what is seen depends upon the interest as well as the skill of the observer.

There is no perfect observational instrument even in physical terms, and when there is a question of looking at anything as fluid and elusive as the emotions, it is obvious that certain features will stand out according to the degree of attention that one gives them. I myself have always been interested in the relationship between emotional and mental states and the well-being of the individual, and therefore I relate what I see to this general question.

The emotional aura has often been called the "astral body." I do not particularly like the phrase, although there is some justification for using it. First of all, the aura has a degree of materiality, and it is localized around a person. Therefore it is a kind of "body." It is "ours" in the sense that during our lifetime we are never without an aura, but its structure, colors and contents can change quite rapidly, so that from year to year our auras might be dramatically different. And finally, it is shining, or starry—thus "astral."

Size

The aura is an ovoid of many-colored light interpenetrating and surrounding the physical body, and extending out from it to a distance of about twelve to eighteen inches. The material of which it is made is very elastic, and thus the aura can expand beyond its usual limits to a considerable degree, depending upon the discharge of emotional energy. Ordinarily, the aura extends about half the distance the arm can reach, although people vary enormously. The reason for this is that some individuals are more inward-turned and others are expansive and outgoing.

The effort to reach out and communicate with others always makes the aura expand. For example, in the case of nurses and doctors, their attention and efforts are directed at helping patients; teachers try to reach their students not only intellectually but with the kind of energy which can engage interest and attention; parents go out to their children with affection and concern.

In the case of musicians, actors, lecturers, politicians, and so on, their auras expand during a performance, but would be at all times larger than average, since their professions make it necessary for them to relate to people in large groups. I suppose that performers unconsciously try to establish a rapport with all the members of their audiences, even those who are sitting in the very rear of the auditorium. This effort creates an expansion of the aura. In lesser degree, we all do the same thing whenever we try to communicate with another person, whether to make a point, to share a joke, or just go out in simple friendship and affection. Elasticity is therefore a basic characteristic of the aura.

Generally speaking, however, there are great differences among people with respect to the size of their auras, and one cannot say what the norm is. This should be kept in mind when looking at the portraits, for although they have been painted uniformly the same size, this was done as a matter of convenience, and is not at all the case in real life.

The aura is tenuous at the edges, merging gradually into the general field, so that the emotions flow outward freely. However, when people are sick their pain and anxiety tend to close them in upon themselves; such a condition can be seen in subjects #15 and #17. The plates might give the impression that in these cases the edges of the aura are inhibiting the outgoing action, but in actuality an artificial boundary is created because part of the emotional energy flow turns inward instead of being released outward in the normal way. This is caused by the fact that their illness so drains them of energy that they can no longer relate to others easily and spontaneously. I have been asked a question which is difficult to answer: what holds the human aura together, and keeps it from dissipating into the general astral field? I can only say that I believe it is held together in much the same way as the physical body is during life: by the presence of the self, which is the principle or center of integration both of the physical systems of the body and of the higher dimensions of consciousness.

Certainly when consciousness departs at death the physical body swiftly disintegrates — and the aura withdraws. Even if we do not admit the presence or absence of the self, we still have to acknowledge that some integrating factor disappears, and without it the body loses its coherence and breaks down. Although the time scale is very different, the situation with respect to the astral body or aura is similar, for it persists after death, gradually disintegrating only as the self or soul withdraws to higher states of consciousness.

I have also been asked whether the aura is subject to the force of gravity or to the earth's magnetic field. These are difficult questions, and I can only say that if there are such effects I believe it is because the aura is tied to the physical body, which is subject to these forces. Certainly the aura has directionality: it has a top and a bottom, and there is a difference between the inner and outer parts, and between the front and the back — but here, again, the physical body is the determining factor. Beyond this, I believe that the principle of resonance which I have already mentioned is important in the composition and coherence of the aura and its relation to the mental and intuitional levels. And resonance results from the fact that the vibrational frequency of the emotional field responds harmonically or sympathetically to the energy states of all the other fields.

In trying to describe the appearance of the personal emotional field, the only analogy I can think of is dense light. These two words are not usually combined, but taken together they can perhaps serve as a metaphor for the aura. As I said in Chapter III, the emotional field is a translucent and transparent medium, for light shines through it. However, its transparency is unlike any other, because the light comes from within, not from without — it is self-luminous. But what is the justification for calling it "dense"? I use this word to try to convey the idea that it is palpable.

Perhaps this idea becomes less strange if we think of a sunbeam when dust motes have gathered the light into a ray, or when, after a shower, the evanescent colors of a rainbow transform everything they touch. So possibly a better analogy would be that the aura looks like a luminous water-vapor — a rainbow-tinted cloud of light.

The other day I was awakened at dawn to find the whole sky flushed with color. I thought it was really very like an aura, which, like the sky at sunrise and sunset, is filled with many hues. It seems dense because it is opaque enough for us to see it, yet we can also sometimes see through it. This is the best description of the aura I can achieve.

Texture and Patterns

However, some emotions are certainly "denser" than others. What I mean by this is that their colors appear to be coarser and muddier. The astral energies which are closely related to the physical body — i.e., emotions which are linked to sense experience, such as cravings and appetites of various kinds — are "heavier" and more granular in texture, as well as slower in their rates of vibration. Whether for this reason or not, they are found in the lowest parts of the aura. These energies are unstable and subject to rapid change; they affect physical states like blood pressure, which can vary over short periods of time. Negative emotions such as resentment, selfishness and greed also tend to sink towards the bottom of the aura, though they may be reflected higher up.

I have said that one of the most striking characteristics of the aura is its dynamism, which allows it to undergo rapid changes in accordance with a person's moods. Nevertheless the aura is not without a durable structure. Just as all human beings share certain physical attributes in common, no matter how different they may appear, so the auras of all of us have certain features in common, even though there may be great variations from one to the other, and some elements may be obscured because of ill health.

The really equable person is something of a rarity, and most of us go through periods of anger, anxiety, disappointment, sorrow or depression from time to time. Unless the condition is pathological, however, these emotional states are usually temporary and pass out of the aura. They are very real to us at the time, but they do not change our fundamental character unless they recur over and over again.

Our stable patterns are more important, because whether we are aware of it or not, some feelings are habitual in us, repeated many times almost every day. The regular recurrence of these emotions makes it easy for us to slip into them unconsciously; thus they become habit patterns which can be perceived in the aura as the background of the more fleeting feelings which are constantly changing during the day. It is these patterns which give one an idea of the basic personality traits a person has developed during a lifetime.

Colors of the Aura

I have observed that everyone comes into this world with a few basic colors. Through the years, I have learned that these colors indicate fundamental personality characteristics incipient in that individual at birth, although they may or may not be allowed to develop later in life. Since no life is predetermined, events will alter this development; circumstances may be so difficult that it is impossible for a per-

Colors of the Emotions

In the emotional field, the spectrum of colors approximates that of the physical world, but with a range of hue, tone, brilliance and subtle blending far beyond what we experience in the physical world. Just as our emotions are "colored" with all kinds of personal responses, attitudes and idiosyncrasies, so the colors of our emotions reflect these admixtures. Thus the rose of affection can be modified to an almost infinite degree: by a tinge of possessiveness or jealousy on the one hand, or by sympathy, kindness and generosity on the other. The colors below, therefore, indicate the basic emotions, and are subject to endless variation.

Scarlet, bright and strong	*anger, irritation*
Rose, light or medium	*love, affection*
Blue, very dark	*will power*
Blue mixed with gray	*strain*
Blue, light sky blue	*religious or other devotion*
Blue, royal	*used in healing for pain reduction*
Blue-green	*aesthetic appreciation, artistic expression*
Green	*work, action*
Green, yellowish	*mind in action*
Yellow, golden	*mind, understanding*
Purple, dark	*meditation with a goal, prayer*
Lavender	*spiritual aspiration and intuition*
Orange	*pride, self-esteem*
Brown	*selfishness, self-centeredness*
Gray	*depression, lack of energy*

For example, a plumber and a musician both work with their hands, and therefore both would have a broad green band, but the difference in the kind of work they do would be reflected in the differences in the shades of green in the two bands. For a pianist, music is not only an aesthetic experience or an intellectual accomplishment; it also represents a great deal of training, discipline and hard work. All this will show itself in the shade and width of the green band.

In many of the pictures you will see various symbols and geometric forms in the green bands, and even faces. Although this area of the aura represents one's work in the world, or sphere of activity, these symbols do not necessarily reflect what a person is thinking about from day-to-day. They seem to stand for something more fundamental and enduring in our lives and actions — our basic attitudes and long-term interests. Sometimes they signify an event or an episode that has been extremely important or influential. Sometimes they embody in symbolic form those contents of our unconscious minds which remain in the background of our thinking and influence our action. They usually remain for quite a long time, gradually changing and evolving only when we alter our fundamental interests and attitudes.

Upper and Lower Hemispheres of the Aura

The "equator" in the aura, as the green band could be called, seems both to link and to differentiate the qualities of that part of the aura which is more deep-seated and enduring (the top) from the part that is involved in the on-going processes of life and the passage of time (the bottom). On the whole, the upper hemisphere is much less volatile than the lower, but it can and does change during the course of a lifetime. When potentialities are developed, the colors deepen and become more brilliant; when unfulfilled, they fade and become dimmer. If one were to completely change one's orientation and, for example, renounce one's religion, the colors related to religious devotion would fade away, and other colors would begin to replace them.

I have said that the lower hemisphere reflects those qualities and emotions which are active in us at the moment. But it also retains the results of our early experience, that is, the past events in our lives insofar as these continue to influence us, consciously or unconsciously. The colors which appear in the mid-portion of this area (that is, from the waist to the knees) represent the feelings we normally use, but deep down in the aura, extending well below the feet, are to be found the residues of our past experience.

Memories of traumatic events and painful experiences, long-lasting fears, anxieties and sorrows — all these sometimes linger at the bottom of the aura, lasting for many years and influencing our behavior in subtle ways. If we stop to think about it, the past itself is gone — only the feelings which are attached to our memories persist into the present. When our circumstances, interests and activities change, the past loses its hold upon us, and then the traces of those memories begin to disappear from our auras.

Emotional Patterns

Sudden surges of powerful emotion, such as fear or anger, can temporarily suffuse the aura from top to bottom, but such feelings usually pass away without changing the general configuration of the emotions. However, when people are overcome by long-lasting grief or depression, this can obscure their usual emotions for a considerable period of time, with the result that their emotional energies are drained and deadened.

From my experience, I have found that most of us are not aware of how much we are affected by what we habitually think and feel. We usually believe that only our physical actions have consequences. While this is true in one sense, from another point of view thoughts and feelings are actions that also have consequences — this time, in terms of our own characters. When I look at a person's aura, I see quite clearly the results of such internal responses. This implies that from moment to moment we are what we experience, and how we respond to that experience. Such a way of seeing ourselves is quite different from the deterministic attitude which holds that personality is the result of a combination of genetic factors and conditioning. What it means is that we can and do change as we alter our habitual responses to our life situations.

We ourselves are influenced and modified by what we think and feel, and in turn our thoughts and feelings are responsive to our experience. There is some truth in the dictum "I think, therefore I am," though not in the sense originally intended. It is not that our existence depends on our thinking, but rather that the thoughts which are habitual in us gradually shape and mold our character. But this is not all there is to it, for we can have control over the process if we so intend. "I am, therefore I think and feel, and what I think and feel reveals what I am," would perhaps be nearer to the mark, for the movement is reciprocal.

Violence

Today there is growing recognition of the damaging effects of watching scenes of violence on films and television. Even so, we do not fully appreciate the extent of this baleful influence. Children are particularly susceptible. When we constantly witness such scenes, it creates in us a tacit acceptance and tolerance of violence. This in turn makes us more prone to give way to tendencies toward violence which may be latent within us (and few of us are totally free from such tendencies). Then when we are exposed to chaotic situations we are less able to resist being overwhelmed by them.

This is why the practice of visualization and meditation has long-term benefits. When we establish a process in ourselves which regularly generates feelings of peace, love and harmony, these feelings become habitual in us, and eventually govern our responses to the world and to the people around us. I shall discuss this process in detail in later chapters.

To repeat, the lower part of the aura expresses the field of our experience—our emotional life as it is lived from day to day—and it therefore portrays what we are feeling at this point in time. This fact should be kept in mind when looking at the aura portraits that follow, for in some cases what one sees is partly the result of temporary conditions.

Organs of Astral Energy Exchange

The emotions have a very powerful effect upon us, even when we are unaware of it. People often think they are completely calm, whereas in reality they are in a state of suppressed turmoil. We know that we live in a physical world that impacts us at every moment, bombarding us with sights, smells and sounds as well as with many unseen forces in the atmosphere. Similarly, at the astral level we are constantly interacting not only with the emotional field as a whole but also with the personal fields of the people with whom we come into contact.

In many ways this interaction can drain us of energy, upset us and make us nervously exhausted, or even unbalance us if we are not stable. But just as we have a physical immune system which helps the body resist invasion, so we have a rejection mechanism at the emotional level which throws off undesirable or negative feelings. This rejection mechanism is a feature common to all of us, and therefore it can be thought of as an organic part of the aura's anatomy.

You will see in the illustrations a number of small cone-shaped vortices placed symmetrically around the edges of the auras. To my knowledge these have never been described elsewhere, but I perceive them as functioning in the energy exchange between the individual and the emotional field as a whole. Over the years I have often referred to these organs without finding any really satisfactory name for them. The best thing I can do is to identify them as valves which take astral energy into the aura from the general field, and then expel it. In other words they are something like organs of respiration that rhythmically "breathe in" and "breathe out" emotional energy, controlling the process of absorption and rejection.

In a healthy individual, this exchange is an automatic process that keeps the emotional energy circulating and replenishes it when it is temporarily depleted by fatigue. But there is a further refinement in the process. The sea of emotional energy that surrounds us at all times contains many disharmonious, negative and even violent elements. I have spoken before of the principle of resonance that governs much of the interaction that takes place between fields. In the case of the aura or individual emotional field, we resonate to those aspects of the general field which are consonant with our own emotional nature. Thus a naturally happy and cheerful individual will automatically reject negative emotions such as depression and anxiety.

This rejection principle is a function of the astral energy valves, and it prevents us from being unconsciously dominated by the emotions of other people, even when we are ill or fatigued. The valves are really a protective mechanism which works automatically to preserve our emotional balance. However, when we are weakened by illness the valves open wider than is normal in order to take in more energy (as in plates #15 and #16), and this causes them to lose a degree of control. When this happens, the rejection process is to some extent impaired, and as a result we are more vulnerable to the feelings of others, less able to throw off negative emotions. Illness thus can cause us to become emotionally sensitive or easily upset, and less resistant to the encroachment of negative feelings like depression or anxiety. These emotions in turn impact our ability to take in prana (vitality) and to function well at the etheric level. This is one reason why people who are ill in hospital should not be subjected to the pressures of too many visitors.

I should mention that in the pictures the size of these valves has been exaggerated in order to make them more visible, and that in real life they are considerably smaller in proportion to the aura.

Emotional Scars

Most of us go through a number of difficult experiences during our lives, but we usually get over them after a while, so that very little memory of the experience is left. When the experience has been really traumatic, however, it can leave a very damaging impression which can easily surface again when a comparable situation calls it forth. In such cases, we never seem to be able to escape from the effects of the experience because everything conspires to remind us of it. Thus we fall progressively into a pattern of emotional repetition.

It is this repetition that creates what I call emotional scars, which are whirls of denser energy in the aura — a record which remains even when we are not consciously thinking about the conflict which caused it. Their position in the aura shows the degree to which the experience is drawn upon in the present: the nearer the green band they appear, the more active they are. For example, if we have made a difficult decision which is opposed by people who are trying to frustrate us, this can create a conflict which does not go away, because there has been no fundamental resolution of the problem. It will therefore create a scar in the region just below the green band.

Experiences even long in the past can continue to exert considerable influence over us, since their results are present in us to a greater extent than we realize. To the degree that our memories are capable of giving us pain or pleasure, they are still active in us. Moreover, we seldom appreciate how often certain feelings and reactions rise up in us over and over again. If we are unhappy about something we tend to dwell on it, and this perpetuates our involvement in the experience. Strengthened by recurring emotion, these memories tend to consolidate into symbols or scars which often look like whorls or shells, for it is their tendency to turn in upon themselves. These symbols often appear to be quite firm and solid, for they are "fed" by the emotional energy generated when we brood over an experience.

Configurations of this kind are a record both of what we have felt in the past and what we are still feeling in the present, and they usually represent an experience which has aroused very strong emotions. However, when we have finally resolved a dilemma or recovered from an emotional shock, we no longer feel impelled to dwell upon it. We have freed ourselves from the memory.

When this happens, the scar which represented the conflict begins

The Chakras

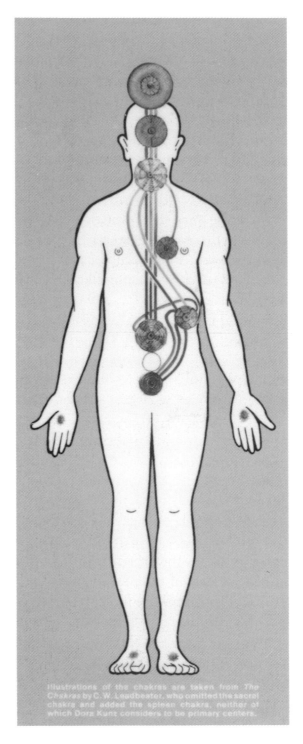

Illustrations of the chakras are taken from *The Chakras* by C. W. Leadbeater, who omitted the sacral chakra and added the spleen chakra, neither of which Dora Kunz considers to be primary centers.

slowly to dissolve, and the energy it contained gradually passes out of the aura. However, if we repeat an emotion such as anxiety or fear day after day, that action will manifest not in the form of a scar but rather as an inhibiting pattern in the personal aura. This is such a widespread problem that I shall discuss it at length in Chapter IX.

It is also possible to have had a wonderful experience so long ago that its memory is no longer vivid, yet it still remains like a lingering fragrance. Although such a memory might be a source of joy and happiness, it would also be represented as a symbolic "scar," this time in the upper part of the aura. In such a case, it could be helpful and inspiring, especially if its meaning is understood. (A good example of such a symbol can be seen in case #12.)

Emotional scars do not necessarily have long-term negative effects. If, having become aware of the problem that has bothered us so long, we really feel that we now understand its causes and have finally outgrown it, such an experience can be very beneficial. That is why all the religions stress forgiveness. This advice is actually very good therapy. If we can say, "I've learned something, and although I can't really love those who have injured me, I am capable of forgiving and wishing them well," then that is the beginning of freedom from bondage to a painful memory.

The Chakras

One very important feature of the anatomy of the aura has been entirely omitted from the pictures because of the difficulty of reproduction. This is the emotional chakra system. Chakras do of course exist at the emotional and mental levels, as well as the etheric, but it would have been too confusing to try to superimpose them upon the other features of the aura. The transparency of astral matter makes it possible to see both back and front of the aura simultaneously, as well as all the intervening features, but it would have been hopeless to try to reproduce this without distortion. Nevertheless, the chakras are an intrinsic part of the anatomy of the aura, and therefore a diagram is included to show where they are placed in relation to the physical body.

A detailed discussion of these centers may be found in my book, *The Chakras and the Human Energy Fields*, to which I have already referred. But for the sake of those who may not be familiar with the function of these organs, I will give a brief overview, beginning with a quotation from the book just cited:

"The chakras are superphysical centers or organs through which the energies of the different fields are synchronized and distributed to the physical body. They are more or less active on the astral, mental and (to some extent) even higher levels . . . but they are of primary importance at the etheric level, where they serve as instruments for the focusing of energy in the body." (p.33)

The primary source of information about the chakras is to be found in Hindu and Buddhist Tantrism, where the psychological foundations of the doctrine of the chakras have been carefully developed. Unfortunately, the symbolic systems upon which these explanations rest require considerable knowledge of their philosophical and religious basis, and therefore most Westerners rely on commentaries, or the testimony of clairvoyant observation. There are a number of books of the latter kind, the earliest and best-known being *The Chakras*, by C. W. Leadbeater.

Stated as simply as possible, the chakras (or "wheels") are organs of consciousness and energy within the personal aura. The major centers, as we often call them, are usually described as seven in number—located at the crown of the head, brow, throat, heart, solar plexus, spleen (or genital region) and base of the spine. They serve as linking mechanisms between the personal fields (etheric, emotional, mental, etc.)—distributing energy as it is needed for different functions—and also between the personal aura and the general emotional field. There is thus a multidimensional relationship among the chakras.

It would not be correct to say that every emotion is reflected in the chakras, for they are not easily influenced. If a person is continually bombarded with strong and disruptive feelings, this might affect the chakras to some degree, but the greatest impact would be on the aura itself. It is the cumulative strength of the emotions, the dominant tone of a person's emotional life, that is represented in the chakras.

At the emotional level, each of these centers has its own special functions, but it is at the same time an integral part of the whole chakra system at that level. The same is true for the etheric centers. But since the two systems are integrated, changes in the emotional field impact the etheric, and in this way can influence physical health. The higher dimensions of consciousness are both more energetic and more stable than the denser fields, such as the etheric — which may seem like a contradiction in terms but is nonetheless true. Therefore, while one could say that the flow of emotional energy reaches the physical body through the connections between the etheric and emotional chakra systems, it is equally true that both the governor and the source of these energies lie at deeper, more stable levels.

The interactions between the various chakras are thus quite complex. Although each chakra has its own functions related to the whole system, within this system certain centers have especially intimate connections. One such coupling involves the solar plexus, the heart and the brow; another links the heart, the brow and the crown chakras. I should mention in addition that there are small, subsidiary centers in the palms of the hands and the soles of the feet. Although these are not part of the major chakra system, they are important in health and healing.

When emotions hit us hard, the heart and brow chakras react, but the primary effects are usually felt in the solar plexus, which is very responsive to the feelings of others. It is here that disturbed emotional energy can directly impact the body, especially in the region of the digestive tract. Anger and jealousy, for example, are explosive and use up much more energy than other emotions; consequently they can quickly drain the energy from the solar plexus, leaving the person limp and exhausted. However, these emotions usually pass out of the aura fairly quickly. Anxiety and depression work more slowly and insidiously, but they can be even more debilitating because they sap the energy of the whole chakra system over a considerable period of time. The resulting stress reacts on the adrenal glands, and may in time even affect the body's immune system.

The Higher Chakras

The crown chakra, the highest in the system, is an organ which is involved in all the ranges of consciousness, from minute variations in brain function to the loftiest spiritual experience. It is therefore the dominant chakra, of such importance that in some traditions it is not even included in the regular chakra system, but is held apart from and above all the rest. In my view, the heart is equally important, for the two working together govern what is most essential in a human being—life and consciousness. For this reason, these are the chakras which are most resistant to damage. Of course if a person has heart disease this will show up in the fluctuating luminosity of that chakra, but if the person is peaceful and well-integrated, the center will be otherwise normal. Here again, it is the sum total of a person's emotions that affects the chakras.

The heart chakra is expansive, opening up with an outpouring of energy whenever we feel love and sympathy. This center is related to all the higher, more unselfish aspects of love, but it is also very responsive to other emotions, such as sorrow, concern for others, elation or depression. The reason is that, due to their close connections, disturbed energy which is centered in the solar plexus can rise up into the heart chakra. This center is extremely important in health, for as I have said, it is the seat of life. It is connected with the thymus gland and through it with the immune system, thus affecting the whole body. On a higher level, the heart is a center of spiritual energy (closely related to the crown chakra) and of personal integration—etheric, emotional and mental, as well as spiritual.

Three of the higher chakras—crown, brow and heart—are linked with all creative endeavor, as well as with self-expression, while the throat and the solar plexus play an important role in emotional projection. The throat chakra is especially involved in human interactions, and with the effort to reach out and communicate with others. It is therefore prominent in teachers, musicians, actors and performers of all kinds.

The creativity with which the brow chakra is involved is not necessarily confined to excellence in the arts and sciences. It is rather the kind of creativity which expresses itself in new ways of thinking, in practical uses of the imagination, in the ingenuity which is able to break stereotypes and invent better ways of doing things. Such creativity can manifest itself in almost any field — business, industry, politics and education, as well as art, science and technology. The ability to relate convincingly with others, which results from the aura's capacity to expand rapidly, is enhanced when there is a good synchronism between the brow and solar plexus chakras. This gives the power of personal projection.

In all these interactions there is a kind of reciprocity. The activity of the chakras makes creative self-expression easier and more natural, and the exercise of this ability in turn stimulates the chakras. For example, since the crown chakra is primarily involved in consciousness, it expands through meditation and becomes more luminous. The brow chakra is also affected, particularly by the kind of meditation that uses a great deal of visualization, or by other disciplines which emphasize focused attention. Thus meditation stimulates the three higher chakras, and in turn the enhanced activity of the chakras energizes and harmonizes all the fields, including the body itself.

Aesthetic experience, that is, response to beauty whether in nature or art, also expands our consciousness and makes us reach out empathically to what we are experiencing. Here both the brow and the heart chakras are active: the brow since it is associated with perception, and the heart because its expansive nature unifies us with other aspects of the world.

Many people have raised questions as to whether the individual chakras can be directly influenced by healing and other practices. I have said that meditation does have such an effect, but this is because the practice is harmonious with the functions of the chakras themselves. It is important to remember not only that the chakras have their special functions, but also that they have their own internal order. Like everything else in the emotional field, these centers may be changed by the disease process, as well as by what we think and feel over a period of time. But if we want to affect the chakras directly we must do so within the parameters of their own order, and this is not an easy thing to do. Unfortunately, some people seem to think that it is possible to stimulate the chakras quite quickly and with fairly simple procedures, whereas in truth it is difficult and takes a consistent, long-term effort.

Kundalini

A number of books have been written about the possibility of "raising" kundalini, an energy concerned with the higher reaches of consciousness. Descriptions of this force, which are mainly to be found in Tibetan and Indian Tantrism, say that the kundalini is latent in the root chakra at the base of the spine. In most people it is unawakened, and authorities agree that it should remain so until the individual has by means of disciplinary practices succeeded in freeing himself or herself from selfish desires. The kundalini is often called the Serpent Fire, because the Goddess "more subtle than the fibre of the lotus, and luminous as lightning, lies asleep coiled like a serpent . . . and closes with her body the door of Brahman [that is, the highest or crown chakra, which is the door to higher consciousness]."[1] When this fire is aroused, it flashes like a bolt of lightning up the spinal cord through all the centers, thereby stimulating them to new levels of activity. But if the kundalini is prematurely awakened in one who is otherwise unprepared, the effects can be quite painful.

---

1. *Tantra of the Great Liberation*, by Artur Avalon, Dover Publications, N.Y., 1972, p.lviii.

Here again, the task of affecting the associated center is (fortunately) far from easy, and if it is to be successful, the whole chakra system must be involved. I have had the good fortune to make the acquaintance of a high Tibetan lama who has practiced meditation from earliest childhood. He is very interesting to me, because he is one of the few people I have ever observed in whom the whole chakra system, including the kundalini, was working as a harmonious, integrated whole.

I am sure that this is due not only to his natural talents but also to the fact that, in the Tibetan tradition, he has had to undergo years of the most rigorous training and discipline. The result is that he has genuine insight and wisdom, and at the same time he is able to project his ideas to others and thus assume the role of leadership. The remarkable thing is that he is completely simple and unassuming, and never gives the impression that he thinks of himself as a superior being.

In his case, all the chakras are fully active and working together as a harmonious whole. As a result, he is a thoroughly integrated human being.

Personal Integration

I have tried in different ways to convey the close interconnections which exist between the different dimensions of consciousness. Even though I describe the emotional aura as a separate entity, it must always be remembered that it is impossible to separate feeling from its mental associations, or thinking from its emotional content. This close interaction between mind and emotion, which is based on the principle of resonance, is both natural and normal.

But there are many people in whom the mind and emotions do not work together well, and then the lack of synchronism causes a dysfunction or aberration. Some of those who live an intense life of the mind are afraid of the emotions, and feel that it is only while engaged in intellectual pursuits that they are free from the demands of others. Such people are often emotionally handicapped.

The aura expands and contracts with our moods, interacts and interpenetrates the auras of others, and yet it always remains a unity. This unity is not achieved by means of the emotional energy alone, but rather through its interconnections with the physical and the etheric, as well as with the higher fields. The etheric establishes physical patterning; one might say that within it the genetic history is summed up. Yet the emotions have a very powerful effect upon the physical body also, for they can be depressing or stimulating. In short, it is the interrelationships among all these dimensions that make us unique individuals, different from one another.

In addition we are all being conditioned by the physical events which constantly impact us, and to which we respond in various ways. Therefore it is not enough to be endowed with great powers of concentration or imagination or creativity; if these talents are to flower they must be used. In this way our experiences in the physical world change us radically, and make us loving or angry, creative or frustrated. Our karma brings us into the world with certain endowments and places us in certain situations. But our freedom lies in what we make of them.

In a well-balanced person, there is symmetry between the upper and lower parts of the aura, the colors which appear above the green band being reflected below it. This shows that the person is using his or her emotional resources fully. The degree to which this reflection is faithful depends upon the person's ability to express these qualities in life—to live them out.

In such a case, the colors all reach the edges of the aura, since the emotions are being expressed freely. What is even more important, the colors would be focused in the heart, which, as I have said, is the center of consciousness—not in the sense of being the focus of our thinking, but as the point of self-integration. It is here that all the energies come together and the individual is harmonized with the whole natural order. All the highly developed, spiritual individuals whom I have observed are focused in the heart. I would not call this cosmic consciousness — that is too big a term — but rather a persisting awareness of the unitive or spiritual aspect of the world.

It has been said by scholars of Tibetan Buddhism, such as Lama Govinda, that our basic intention or aspiration, our fundamental purpose in life, is never lost; it is a thread which persists throughout every change. Although Buddhists accept reincarnation, they reject the existence of a permanent self — or even selfhood. I would not try to claim that the self is eternal, but it certainly persists throughout this life and beyond.

To me, the principle of integration which unites the many dimensions of consciousness and energy within us is this timeless self. Itself unchanging, it is the fundamental cause and source of everything we are and can be.

II
The Cycle of Life

V
The Development of the Individual

The aura is at once a representation of our innate character, an indication of our potentials, and a record of our experiences. In the case of a child, the first two are present, but the experiences all lie in the future, and therefore there are great differences between the auras of an adult and of a baby or small child. I have tried to make clear the fact that at the level of the emotions an individual's basic character is continually undergoing the effects of experience, and that the dynamics of daily life will in the long run bring forth potentialities, or suppress them.

As adults, we have lived through many different kinds of experience, some of which have given us mixed feelings of success or failure, happiness or pain. As a result, we are often ambivalent about what has happened, and this ambivalence creates uncertainties and dissonances in the aura. Few of these appear in very young children, whose auras are usually clear and uncomplicated. As the baby grows into the child, potentials begin to unfold, experiences of the outside world impinge, and the aura undergoes various stages of transformation. As might be expected, the auras of small children change quite rapidly, in pace with their physical and mental development.

As you will see in the pictures that follow, the baby comes into the world with certain innate characteristics which are in a sense enfolded within the aura like tightly closed buds. These incipient abilities begin to show themselves quite early in life, as the child interacts with others and begins to explore its world. Musical talent, for example, flowers very young, and on a lesser scale, a child's quickness to learn as well as its affection and ability to relate to others soon manifest themselves.

These basic predispositions and talents are potentialities which are available to the child, but whether they develop fully in later life depends upon many factors. Personal relationships, motivation and interest, as well as karmic conditions like opportunity, all play a part.

The Skandhas

Today it is customary to relate innate abilities to genetic factors. I do not question the importance of these factors, but all my life I have accepted the fact of reincarnation, and from my observations of babies and children, I feel sure that the experiences of a previous life also play a part in this one. Each person comes into the world with certain attributes, or *skandhas*, as the Buddhists call them: "conditions of existence" which we all bring with us at birth. While these are obviously connected with genetic factors, there is also a basic, unique individuality which is sometimes strangely different from the family pattern, with unaccountable idiosyncrasies. We know that during life the present is shaped for an individual by past experiences; reincarnation merely extends this past to include a larger heritage of assimilated experiences.

As we shall see when we discuss the auras of children, the concepts of reincarnation and karma are always linked with the problem of determinism. There are, for example, children who are born with a very open, sensitive constitution which makes them vulnerable to the emotions of others. This is a difficult situation for the child, which will be a test of its character throughout life. The results are not determined, and cannot be foreseen.

The concept of *skandhas* comes closer, I believe, than any other to identifying the causal connection between our past in its entirety and what we now are. You could say that each one of us is "caused" by our heritage—physically, of course, but also mentally and emotionally. But, according to reincarnation, that heritage is not limited to this brief life, but extends far back to the dawn of our consciousness. It equally reaches into the most distant future, for what we are now — which includes the changes we make in ourselves — becomes the seeds of what we shall be. This is the essence of the evolution of consciousness.

Karmic Indicators

The auras of babies and children bear witness to this causal connection with the past; it is represented in the peculiar and mysterious formations which are a feature common to the young, but which disappear when one becomes adult. (See Plates 1, 2 and 3.) These features have bearing upon the future of the individual, so I have called them "karmic indicators" for want of a better phrase. They are very difficult both to see and to describe, because they are involved with different aspects of the time dimension. Our experience of time is of course extremely complex. Since karma is a causal relationship, it is tied to the time factor: it reaches far back into the past and, especially in the case of children, is often discharged much later in life.

As a result of all this, the karmic indicators represent the essence of what an individual will experience in this incarnation and point to the seeds of problems which will be met in the future. But they do not necessarily reveal the situations that will trigger these problems. As I have said, they are in many ways the most difficult of all the features of the human aura to examine and interpret, for they appear to be multi-dimensional. They are concerned with general conditions of the life to come — with problems and difficulties that could take different forms and be worked out in different ways. In other words, they are not specific prescriptions for future events. Thus what one sees within them is not a set of predetermined events a person will inevitably have to face (such as an accident at the age of twenty, for example), but rather the *kinds* of situations that will be encountered during life. This bears out my statement that karma is not deterministic.

Such situations often come to us unsought but they have to be con-

The Skandhas

In Buddhism, the human personality or individuality has been defined as made up of five "heaps" or "bundles of attributes," which are usually categorized as the senses, feelings, perceptions, volition, and pure consciousness or awareness.

Lama Govinda points out that the skandhas *cannot be regarded as separate parts, out of which an individual is composed, but only as different aspects of an indivisible process, for, according to the Pali Canon: "What one feels, that one perceives, and what one perceives, that one is conscious of."[1]*

The personal self is said to be impermanent, since like all phenomena, it is dependent on the process of lawful change, or the principle of causality. Arising from this principle, the theory of karma, which balances present circumstances against the results of past actions, holds that our present life is due to the impressions of the karma of the past life, and that it will in turn shape our future. As Lama Govinda describes it:

"Just as a potter creates the shapes of pots, so we form our character and our destiny, or, more correctly, our karma, the outcome of our deeds in works, words and thoughts. . . . Skandhas, *the group of mental formations . . . as a result of those volitional acts, become a cause of new activity and constitute the actively directing principle or character of a new consciousness."[2]*

"From this follows the dynamic nature of consciousness and existence, which can be compared to a river which, in spite of its continually changing elements, keeps up the direction of its movement and preserves its relative identity. . . . [This is] the stream of existence or, more correctly, of becoming — in which all experiences or contents of consciousness have been stored since beginningless time, in order to reappear in active, waking consciousness whenever the conditions and mental associations call them forth."[3]

1. *Foundations of Tibetan Buddhism, p.71f*
2. *Ibid., p. 242f*
3. *Ibid., p.73*

fronted, and therefore they are related to the direction our future will take. The freedom lies in the ways in which we meet these situations — whether they offer a challenge to our creativity, or an insurmountable obstacle to our development. How we will respond cannot be foreseen. In trying to interpret the indicators in the auras of children, therefore, I have sometimes been wrong in the specifics, but not in the generalities.

"Store Consciousness"

There is another Buddhist teaching which relates to the mysterious nature of these karmic indicators that appear in the auras of children. This is the concept of "store consciousness,"[4] the idea that the whole of one's past experience (both deeds and their fruit) is in some way never lost, but remains stored up at a deep level of consciousness which, though unperceived, is always present in us. (It is perhaps analogous to the ways in which the whole history of our Earth is preserved in its present structure.) Although I do not know to what degree this concept has been developed in Buddhism, from my observation it is a clue to the ways in which karma is accepted by the individual at birth as part of the conditions of that particular life — the pattern which is about to unfold.

So when I see these formations in the aura of a child, I perceive them as the reflections of the seeds of individuality which originate at the deepest level of the self. They go far beyond the inheritance of physical characteristics. It is now acknowledged that the genes carry some emotional predispositions — tendencies towards certain kinds of emotional or mental response. We sometimes see traits of the parents reflected in the children, and this is not necessarily the result of parental influence. One cannot say that they are inherited, but rather that the genetic factors are hospitable to the development of such characteris-

---

4. Please note the final quotation from Lama Govinda on the facing page description of the *skandhas*.

tics: the predisposition is there, as in musical families, where the environment fosters it. All this is represented in the karmic indicators, for of course the family that one is born into is a matter of karma.

In the descriptions of children that follow, everything which I predicted at the time about their future (whether right or wrong, and, as I have said, I was sometimes wrong) was based on my observation of these karmic indicators. On the other hand, such things as temperament, potentialities, and the emotional qualities or personal characteristics of the child show up in the colors of the aura itself.

Potentialities

In looking at the aura of a small child, therefore, I get a general idea of what the child's potentialities will be — whether artistic or intellectual, for example — but I cannot tell how they will develop. I could make mistakes about the ways in which these potentialities will manifest themselves, for they unfold gradually and sometimes never become fully realized in the day-to-day activities and experiences of a person's life. It is here that karma plays a part, for the circumstances in which we find ourselves may not be conducive to the flowering of a talent or predisposition we were born with.

The interaction between mind and emotion, which I have already talked about, is an energy exchange that is always conditioned in some way by an individual's basic pattern, inherent from birth. But this interaction is affected by a person's environment, as for example, a childhood in which emotions have been repressed. There is always in us a mixture of the characteristics we were born with and the conditioning which overlays these characteristics as a result of our experience. This observation almost goes without saying, since it is so widely recognized as the nature-nurture interplay in personality development.

Some people are strong enough to overcome the handicaps with which they were born, and thus can remain unaffected even by a very negative environment. On the other hand, people born with a brilliant intellect may be deeply afraid of their emotions, a condition which is probably the result of their upbringing. So when one sees the shadowy presence of the adult within the child, one cannot say with precision how that presence will eventually emerge, or what its exact features and behavior will be.

Emotional Vulnerability

Some babies and small children are vulnerable to the emotions of others because they cannot as yet understand their causes. If, for example, children are subjected to persistent criticism by their parents, they may easily interpret this as disapproval or rejection, whereas it may in fact arise from the parents' interest and desire that the children should succeed. The effect on a child's emotional field, however, will be to instill a continual state of anxiety, and if this persists for a long period of time it can be very inhibiting.

I have found that many parents do not realize the effects of their own emotions upon their children. If a parent has a sudden flash of anger at a child (which may be entirely justified), the outburst will trigger a momentary strong interaction, but the anger will usually dissipate fairly quickly. But if a parent expresses constant disapproval of the child, this can not only cause resentment but, more importantly, can so undermine the child's self-confidence as to affect it for the rest of its life.

On the other hand, a loving interaction between parents and children is both stabilizing and energizing. It slowly develops a mutual sensitivity and rapport which has lifelong benefits, for it creates an atmosphere of basic trust.

There is one more general comment I should like to make about the auras. When, in the pictures that follow, we see at the top of the aura the bands of light having to do with inspiration or spiritual perception, this is a reflection of the individual's potential, but it also represents the link between that person and the timeless self, or with the spiritual dimension of human consciousness. No matter what name we give it, this aspect of a human being is the bridge to a higher reality in which we are all rooted — a bridge which always exists whether we choose to use it or not.

1. A Mother and Unborn Child

Our first picture represents the aura of a woman of about twenty-two years of age pregnant with a seven-month-old fetus. As you can see, the baby's aura is quite distinct from the mother's, although they are interconnected in various ways.

Let us first take the mother. Her pregnancy has caused changes in her energy patterns, as might be surmised. The energy valves at the edges of her aura are somewhat enlarged, and they are no longer cone-shaped; they have widened at the base and narrowed at the top. These changes have occurred in order to permit her to take in more energy, and also to protect her from other people's emotional disturbances, so that her own rhythm will not be affected. In this way her rejection mechanism works more selectively.

The first general impression of this aura is that it is remarkably clear and uncomplicated. This is partly due to her youth, but to a greater degree to her own nature. As you can see, there is a great deal of pink in her aura, for she was a very loving, giving, sweet girl who was at the moment full of affectionate feelings for her husband and family, and supremely happy to be having a baby. Above the green band the shade of pink is more delicate; it represents her innate capacity for loving response. The large area of a darker pink below the green band reflects the love for her family which dominated her emotions at that time; full of joy at her pregnancy, she was feeling friendly towards the world. This characteristic might not be so prominent in the future.

The large area of pale green in the upper part of her aura opposite the pink indicates that one of her innate qualities was sympathy or empathy, a characteristic which, together with the pink of affection, shows itself in loving kindness and a wish to be helpful to others. You

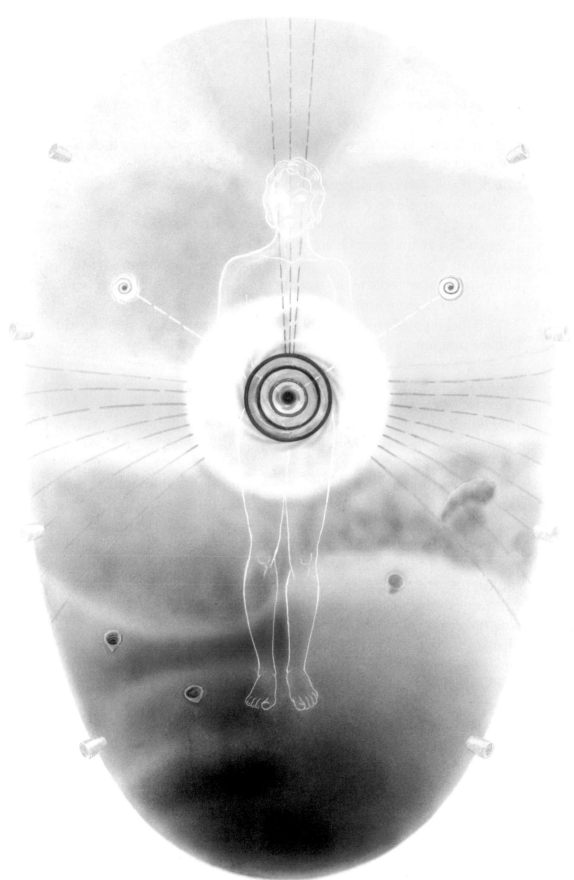

1. A Mother and Unborn Child

will see that the color merges into the yellow which appears high above the head on both sides. Yellow is always the color of the mind; in her case it is not present as intellectual power so much as in her ability to relate to people through a kind of sympathetic understanding. This large area of green high in the aura also embodies qualities of openness, and an attitude which accepts and tries to make the best of things. But it must be remembered that the colors in the upper part of her aura are her potentials (she was after all still very young) as well as what she was expressing at the time.

This girl was a devout Catholic, and went to church every day during her pregnancy. This religious devotion shows itself in the blue extending above her head, and also in the lines of deeper blue which penetrate the baby's aura. These are caused by the prayers she offered daily for the baby's welfare. It is interesting to note that a baby is usually protected quite fully from outside emotional influences, but in this case, the lines of religious feeling penetrate right through its protective shield.

Her green band shows that she was quite practical and capable, but its pale color indicates that she was not using this ability much at the moment. The lines covering the band and descending into the lower part of the aura indicate that her action and interest were all turned inward toward the baby, and that most of her energy was going in this direction. All this would change once the baby was born.

At the bottom of the aura, near and below the feet, one always sees the dark colors which reveal traces of selfishness, for very few of us are completely free of self-interest. In her case there is rather less than usual. It is represented in the streak of brown low down on the left, which results from her occasional feeling that her family is a burden she wishes she could get rid of; it is mixed with the dark blue of strain caused by the fact that she had been forcing herself to keep on working when she did not feel like it. In her case, the separation of the gray, blue, brown and green streaks does not give an accurate picture, for in actuality these colors were mixed together in a cloud-like formation. The difficulty with trying to portray such features of the aura is that it is impossible to mix different pigments together without losing their individual character, whereas in the aura the colors always remain distinct even when they are mixed together.

The patch of gray indicates that her early youth was marred by a time of weariness and depression, complicated by worries about people she was fond of. The fact that she was not entirely free from this worry is shown by the pink whirls to the left of her feet. One of these is somewhat higher up in the aura, within an area of blue, which shows that she was determined to embark on a course of action which might create some conflict with those she was fond of.

On the opposite side of her aura, the large area of yellow-green shows that she had to work while she was quite young. Its grayish tone, particularly toward the bottom, indicates that the work she had to do was dull and monotonous, and also that some of her associations were with people who were inconsiderate and had a depressing effect on her. The gray plume was probably caused by an illness in the not too distant past, which sapped her energy and made her fearful that she might not be strong enough to do everything that was expected of her. But I saw this as only a temporary condition which would pass out of her aura quite soon under the influence of her pregnancy.

Although I had never seen this girl before she sat for us, I could tell immediately that she was fundamentally a strong, healthy, stable and well-balanced girl who exhibited few signs of stress. This is shown by the fact that the clear colors of her lower aura flow right through to the edges. This is remarkable, because I later learned that she had been born in the slums of New York City with no material advantages whatsoever, so that from her early teens she had to work very hard under difficult conditions. Even in childhood she had the responsibility of providing for other members of her family, but she seldom begrudged them the effort involved, and had no resentment whatsoever.

She had very little education and thus few opportunities to develop her mind—a fact which I deduced from the pale color of the yellow and its position high in the aura. But nevertheless she was a sensible girl. In spite of what most people would have considered a hard life, she had no bitterness or self-pity within her, but was instead sweet, simple, cheerful and loving. I have rarely seen anyone with such a giving nature. This was her unique quality.

This is not to say that she was not depressed occasionally, or that she did not have her difficulties. Her circumstances were still poor, and life cannot have been easy for her. She sometimes worried about her baby's future, a concern which shows itself in the gray mixed with the rose-pink in the lower aura. The reddish vortices on the lower left represent little irritations, such as the lack of money, but the fact that these are on the surface rather than more deeply embedded in the aura indicates that they were only temporary and would disappear in a day or two. On the whole, the troubles this girl had suffered in the past had remarkably little permanent effect on her.

One of the most interesting things about this aura is the presence of two configurations which you will see symmetrically placed on either side above the green band. I have already spoken of the kar-mic indicators which appear in the auras of children and foreshadow their future in some mysterious way. In this case, because the baby's karma is still entirely dependent on the mother, these indicators ap-pear in her aura, although they are connected with the baby by lines of energy. When you think of it, this is not so surprising, since they represent the patterning of his future karma and this is not affecting the baby much as yet. And since there is always a karmic link be-tween mother and child, these indicators are also acting indirectly upon her. At the moment of the child's birth, they will vanish from her aura and reappear within that of the baby, as may be seen in the infant's picture which follows this.

At this stage the baby's future is foreshadowed, as it were, by the lines of light which connect the karmic indicators to his aura. As I said before, these configurations represent the tendencies which the baby will have to deal with in the future, and contain images that relate to people and events that lie ahead. In a fetus this close to term, certain patterns are just beginning to be worked into the child's psyche, or emotional field, impregnating it even before he is born, for these patterns are practically unavoidable. (You will notice that I refer to the baby as "he," because in this case I was quite sure that it would be a boy.)

From my point of view, karma—and indeed all our actions—represents releases of energy, but this energy is not necessarily physical. It can be generated at different levels of consciousness. At birth, the soul or self assumes what it will work out—take upon itself—both in the way of constructive energy as well as destructive. Thus the karmic pattern begins to unfold. The mistake we make lies in thinking that destructive or difficult patterns are "evil." Being born with a handicap, for instance, is from the immediate point of view bad karma, but long-term it can represent an opportunity for inner growth.

The actual aura of the baby is represented by the strong, dark, concentric bands of colors in the center of the picture. Surrounding these is an opalescent cloud of delicate colors. This is the protective device I mentioned previously, which shields the baby from emotional shocks and might be thought of as the astral equivalent of the placental barrier. Although it is permeable, especially by higher energies, it protects the baby from the worst effects if the mother should be subject to trauma or to violent emotional swings. In other words, if there were destructive forces within the mother, which is unfortunately sometimes the case, this barrier would prevent them from destroying the astral fetus, although some negative effects might get through.

The yellow in the fetal area does not in this case stand for intellect; it is rather a reflection of the tremendous amount of prana (life energy) that is being poured into the baby. The green lines of force through the middle of the aura are an indication of the energy exchange between the mother and child at the emotional level, but you can see that—unlike the radiant effects of her prayers—they do not penetrate the opalescent cloud which is protecting the baby. In fact, the mother's religious devotion only reaches the baby because it is energy from a much higher level.

Because this picture is a two-dimensional representation of a three-dimensional form, the baby's aura looks like a flat disk, but in reality it is a round globe formed of concentric spheres of color. At its heart there is a central sphere of purple/blue, which represents its focus of energy. This center is linked with the baby's higher self or soul, which at this stage of development is still detached from the baby.

Around this center extend three colored spheres. The innermost one is green, the next is rose, and the outermost is blue, and the whole aura is in continuous pulsating movement. In an unborn child, the aura seems always to be circular in structure and slowly rotating, for the emotions are as yet enfolded, complete in themselves, and do not extend outward into the world of experience.

The colors here are very intense, and this told me that the baby would have a strong and definite personality. The dark shade of green indicates practicality; I predicted that he would be able to accomplish a good deal because his concentration would be in the physical world. The dark rose indicates a deeply affectionate nature, while the strong blue presages an equally strong will and a forceful personality that might on occasion become domineering. The aura throughout is most definite, and indicates a child that will develop into a strong, stable, forceful but kind and affectionate man.

In the case of this baby, I predicted that he would be a ward politician, or occupy some position where he would influence a considerable number of people. I was wrong in this, because I learned much later that he had become a scientist, but in another way I was right, because he did work with the materials of the physical world, where I said his concentration would be. Although I never saw mother or child again, it was reported to me that he had a successful career, and that he became the mainstay of a large family who looked to him for guidance and support.

2. A Seven-Months-Old Baby

Plate 2 shows the aura of a seven-month-old boy, a healthy and vigorous child.

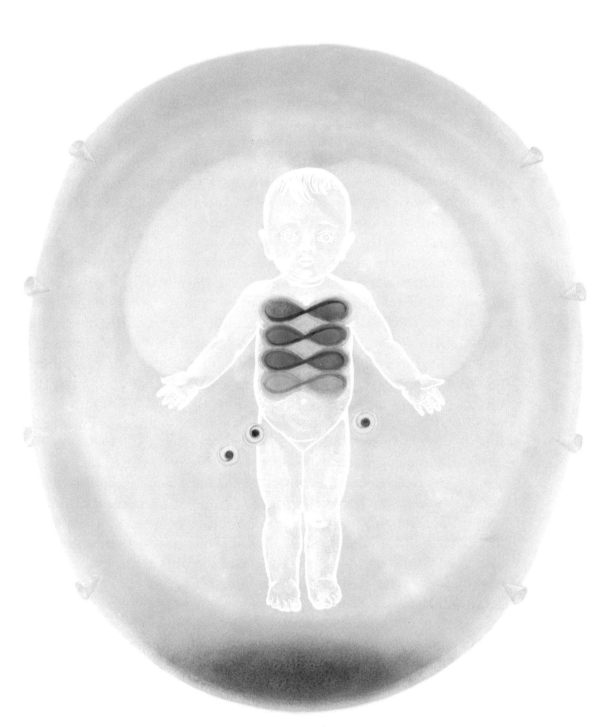

2. A Seven-Months-Old Baby

After birth the aura undergoes certain radical changes. In the unborn child, the whole aura was enfolded within the bands of color which represented his fundamental character traits, for as yet it was without contact with the world of experience. From the moment of birth this situation changes, for with the first breath the baby begins to interact with its environment and to feel this interaction. The basic emotions reorganize themselves and begin the process of unfoldment.

At seven months, this baby was starting to reach out to others, and to respond to this experience. The shape of the aura is in the first stage of transition from the sphere of the unborn child, but its form is still much more rounded than that of an adult. The color distribution is also quite different, for in an infant the shades are difficult to distinguish. They tend to blend and merge with one another, for babies' emotions are very volatile; they can cry one moment and laugh the next. The whole aura has a translucent quality that is difficult to reproduce; it has somewhat the effect of a softly glowing opal, in which flashes of color come and go.

Around the upper part of the body and the head there is an extensive area of yellow, which shows that the baby was beginning to use his mind to explore his environment. Although his powers of thinking were as yet limited, the color shows that he would have a good intelligence. The larger area of pink represents affection; this baby had known nothing but loving care, and the pink represents his free response. He was a strong, lively baby, and on the whole very good-tempered.

The other colors surrounding the top of the aura, pale blue-green and lavender, are vague and undeveloped. They represent the baby's connection with his spiritual background—a semi-conscious presence that broods over all very young children for a period of time.

The green band which is a feature of all adult auras has not yet formed, because the infant has not learned to express himself in the physical world or to exercise any control over his environment. At this age, in fact, the colors of the aura are encapsulated or inward-turned, rather than discharging their energy into the general field. This is in one way a protection for the baby against emotional shocks; in another it is a result of the basic selfishness or self-centeredness (shown in the patch of brown at the bottom of the aura) that is almost a necessary characteristic of all small children, who must develop their sense of ego in order to learn. Very small children think almost entirely in terms of their own wants; as they grow older and reach out to others and to the world around them their auras will open up.

The concentric bands of strong color, which in the unborn child represented its basic characteristics, undergo a transformation at birth. In the baby, they are replaced by a series of small petals or winglike formations, which emerge from the very center of the aura. These petals, which are not really so rigid or definite as they appear in the picture, are a feature of the auras of all very young children; they represent the seeds of the future emotional life and indicate temperament and potential capacities. The number varies from individual to individual; four or five is usual.

Even at so young an age, these capacities were beginning to unfold. At that time they were still close to the body and its energies, but month by month they would expand until they gradually filled the whole of the upper aura. In some babies, one or two of the petals will unfold more quickly than the others, but in this case they were all expanding at the same time.

The lowest of these pairs of petals is a dark green — this baby's green band in embryro, as it were. The shade of color indicates that he would be practical and have his feet on the ground, and also that he would be well-coordinated, with the possibility of developing some physical skills. Just above the green appear two wings of pink. Here the color indicates that he would be affectionate, but somewhat inclined to lose his temper, or be emotionally volatile. There are faint lines of stress in the pink, which indicate that he might be emotionally tense later in life.

The dark blue immediately above the pink is a strong color and shows a considerable amount of potential energy. It indicates a strong will, which he will be able to use to control his emotions and direct his actions, but it also might indicate stubbornness. The strength of all these colors shows that he would always have strong emotions, but the way they are placed suggests that on the whole he would have good control over his feelings. Above the blue, the violet petals give indication of a ritualistic turn of mind, though this would probably be expressed more in the sense of a liking for order and appropriateness in his life, and perhaps an interest in art and aesthetics, though he himself would not be an artist.

In the lower part of the aura may be seen three of the karmic indicators I have spoken of. In one of these there is indication that he would have some emotional problem in which his greatest struggle would be with himself, rather than with others. Within another a number of faces can be seen, showing that his work or profession will necessitate interaction with many individuals, and that he will have to learn to deal with some opposition. The third formation shows a spiritual struggle of some sort.

At the present time (fifty years later), this infant has developed into a very successful businessman, in the prime of life. He has a strong will and good self-control in his dealings with others, even under difficult circumstances (the potential for this was shown by the blue). His temperament is friendly and outgoing, and he is loving and affectionate in his family relationships. The healthy and vigorous baby has grown into a strong man, who is physically well-coordinated, as was predicted. In school and college he participated in many team sports, and he is still an excellent golfer and tennis player. He has also had to face stress and opposition in some of his business associations, as was foreseen in one of his karmic indicators.

One of his less-realized potentials is represented by the purple in the baby's aura. As a young man he was interested in literature and in philosophical ideas, but his circumstances have led him in another direction, and his energies have taken an entrepreneurial turn. His appreciation of art and music remains keen, however, and he is somewhat of a collector of Chinese ceramics. From the beginning, the blue in his aura indicated a strong will and a determination to succeed, and these have not diminished with age. He has directed his considerable intelligence toward making a success of his many ventures, and his energy and drive have led him confidently in a number of different directions.

3. A Four-Year-Old Girl

The aura of a four-year-old child is less round than that of an infant, but it has not yet reached the oval form of an adult. The leaf-like formations of the baby have disappeared, and their colors have dissipated into the aura, forming quite definite bands of green, pink, blue and yellow. These are the primary characteristics of this little girl, which would have been represented in concentric circles in the fetus, and as leaves of color in the baby.

Even at this early age the colors of her aura were bright, an indication that her feelings were and always would be intense, and that her emotional reactions from moment to moment will have great impact on the decisions she makes. She will always have a need to express her feelings, and her personal relationships will be very important to her. The two karmic indicators in her aura (low down, below her knees) confirm that her problems will always be related to individuals with whom she has strong emotional attachments.

Pink is the dominant color in her aura, showing that she was a loving child, and that her nature would always be warm and affectionate. The darker blue which is above the pink indicates the power of will, which was as yet only a potential; whether or not she would use this wisely cannot yet be certain. If used wrongly, she could become stubborn as well as possessive, for the proximity of the blue to the pink indicates that she would be generous but at the same time clinging in her affections. This characteristic might continue throughout her life.

The brown at the bottom of the aura is caused by selfishness of the kind normal in children, who at this age are bent on finding and expressing themselves. Just above it, the incipient blue-green band extends to just below the knees; as she grows older it will move upward toward the middle of the aura. Its shade shows a strong artistic potentiality, and the fact that it deepens in color toward the bottom indicates a vivid imagination, which goes hand in hand with her artistic ability. The width of the green indicates her capacity for putting her thoughts and feelings into action, which at the age of four was just beginning to develop.

The yellow extending across the upper part of the aura and around the head indicates the possibility of a clear mind, which she was just beginning to use. Perhaps surprisingly, yellow shows more prominently in a child of this age than it would a little later on, because curiosity is starting to stimulate thought. But the yellow is amorphous, diffuse and without clarity and precision, none of which could be expected in so young a child. The opalescent rainbow of colors at the very top of the aura is typical of all young children. As I mentioned in connection with the baby's aura, the appearance of such colors is caused by a resonance with the child's spiritual background, which has not yet been obscured or altered by life experience.

This little girl was too young to have developed her potentialities to any great extent, and her aura was just beginning to settle into some kind of pattern. The colors indicating the potentials which I have described were not yet structured into her aura, but were still rather vaguely diffused through it.

A year before this child's aura was painted, her father had been killed in an accident. Even though she had been too small to realize fully what had happened, the trauma shows up in the downward droop of the edges of her aura, including the green band, as well as in the fact that the colors are encapsulated within a pale shell. As yet her emotions show no sign of breaking through this barrier and becoming normally outgoing. Such a condition is not unusual at her age, but was probably aggravated by the loss of her father.

The blue dashes on either side of the pink band were caused by definite emotional strain. There are no signs of inhibition in her affec-

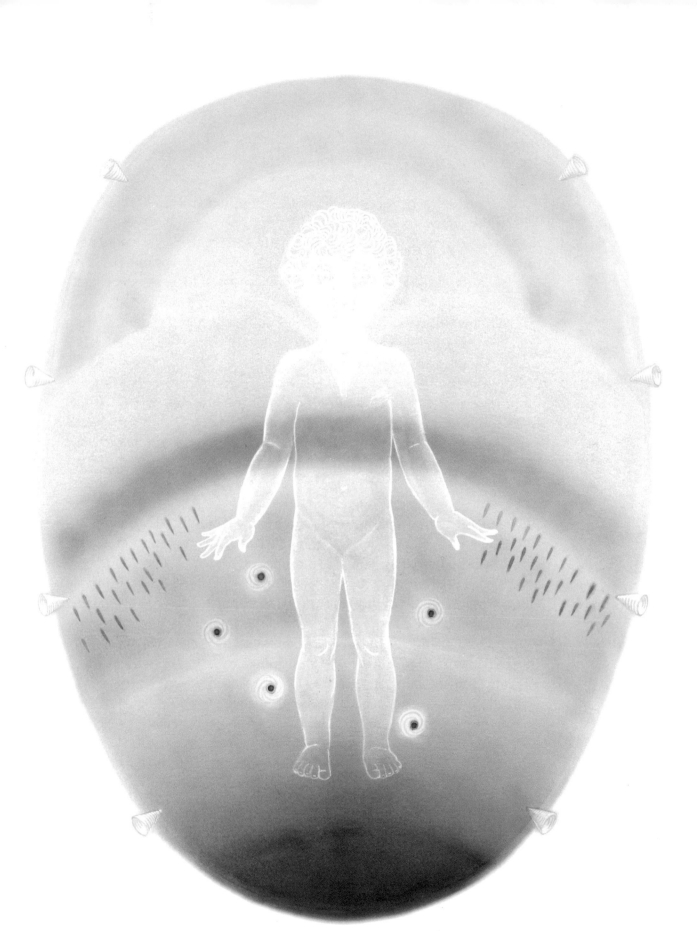

3. A Four-Year-Old Girl

tions, but the blue dashes indicate that she had suffered from stress within the family relationships even before the loss of her father. Normally, these marks would move out of the aura as the stress decreased, but in her case it seems they were fading more slowly. So much strain at such an early age indicates that she had very little sense of security, even though her affections were freely expressed.

I have had an opportunity to see this child again as a grown woman with four children and several grandchildren, and to discuss with her the problems and events of her life.

In maturity, this woman still possesses a feeling for beauty — an aesthetic appreciation — although she has not fulfilled her artistic promise as she might have done. Her innate sense of color, proportion and form, however, continues to influence her responses to her environment. She is repelled by ugliness, and has a talent for creating attractive, harmonious surroundings wherever she lives, even with meager resources.

I felt originally that she would be a person who had a deep emotional need to express her feelings, and now, fifty years later, this characteristic is no longer latent, but fully expressed. Loving and being loved are all-important to her. Because of this, and because people close to her have not always responded to her need, she has often been blocked in her feelings. This has been true even of her relationships with her children. Her nature is to express her feelings freely and spontaneously, but there have been many obstacles to this expression.

Therefore she has had her emotional ups and downs, but through it all she has never lost the warmth of her feelings, or her strong desire to interact with other people; it is a basic necessity of her nature. Not everyone feels this — some people are even afraid of close relationships — but to her they are all-important. Because of this she has often been impulsive in her decisions, and allowed her feelings to dominate her actions. This has led her into some difficult and unhappy situations.

At this moment in her life she has begun at last to find some work that interests her, and part of the energy she always expended in her feelings for others is now finding an outlet in doing something she enjoys. Thus she is not so entirely dependent upon her personal relationships. However, she will never be happy in any kind of work that does not give her an opportunity to interact with others, for even when such contacts are not personal, they to some extent satisfy her need to be involved on a human level.

In addition, her children are no longer dependent upon her, and therefore this relationship has become less intense. She still shows the results of a basic frustration which she experienced over a period of years, but her emotions are becoming less subject to swings from high to low. She is now faced with a difficult personal situation, but since it is being resolved, some of her emotional pressure is relieved.

At present, the color yellow in her aura has both increased in extent and deepened in tone, because for the first time in her life she is trying to think things through, rather than acting upon impulse. I can see that she is beginning to consider what the results of her actions might be, and trying to work out her problems step by step rather than following the dictates of her feelings. As a result, her mind is opening up to new ideas. Religion and the search for her spiritual roots have always played a part in her life, but it is people, not abstract ideas, that are her necessity. Since she lives most intensely in her emotional relationships, she would feel bereft without someone she was close to; she is not the kind of woman who could take pleasure in living alone. She also lives very much in the present and does not cling to the past. This has a positive effect, for although she is very fond of her children and grandchildren, she is not possessive.

At this point in her life, she has genuinely begun to turn her life around. The depression she has suffered as the result of unhappy relationships has not entirely left her, but she is learning from those experiences. The brighter colors are beginning to shine through the depression, and her higher sensitivities are beginning to function in her life. She has matured.

As you can see from this brief account of her life, this woman's emotional nature was established very early, and the tendencies which were revealed in her aura as a young child influenced her life strongly as an adult.

4. A Seven-Year-Old Boy

In the aura of this boy of seven, the mind was beginning to develop actively, along with his other expanding powers. He was full of curiosity about all sorts of things and asked endless questions, but as yet he had little interest in putting ideas to any practical use.

At this age, the aura is starting to take on the ovoid form and structural features of an adult. The green band, which is so important an element in maturity, is starting to take shape, and this shows that the child is beginning to venture into the world and do things on his own. However, this boy's green band does not extend all the way to the edges of his aura, because his ability to carry his ideas through into practice was as yet only incipient. He had not much interest or ability in doing things with his hands, although there are signs that later on, as an adult, he could develop a number of practical skills.

There is already evidence in his aura of his intellectual capabilities, but rather as a reflection of a deeper mental level than as a capacity actually in use. This potential ability shows itself not only by the amount of yellow but also in the shade of the green band, which has a yellowish tinge. The patch of yellow-green on the right side below the band reflects his interest in things, the use of his mind in his school work, his feeling for the meaning of words, and in general his wish to learn and to know things for himself.

At the bottom of the aura, above the usual mottled green-brown of selfishness, there is a kind of reflection of this characteristic in a large patch of greenish-yellow stretching all across the aura. This signifies a self-conscious striving to master the physical world, which manifested as self-assertiveness, a form of egotism which is fairly common in children.

The pink, which extends all across the aura above the green band, shows that he had plenty of affection but that he was not yet the master

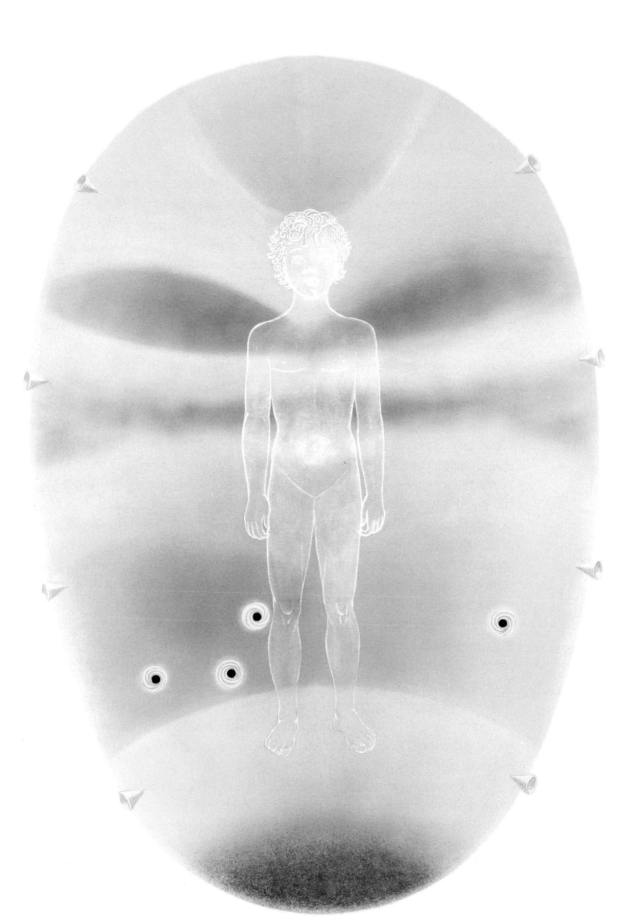

4. A Seven-Year-Old Boy

of his feelings; they were uncertain and still expanding. The dots within the pink indicate emotional struggle and sometimes a loss of temper, but they will fade quickly, since, as in most children, they are only momentary. He was sensitive, and could easily get his feelings hurt. The opalescent colors above represent a kind of idealistic attitude toward people, which may at times make him unrealistic in his expectations about the ways in which they will respond.

The juxtaposition of green, blue-green and yellow in this boy's aura shows that he will develop aesthetic appreciation, but not along the usual lines, for his searching mind will dominate his feelings. This already showed itself in a kind of personal fastidiousness. The seeds of these intellectual abilities are clearly indicated by the shade and amount of yellow in his aura, as well as by the fact that his green band is yellowish in shade. But as yet the colors above the band are not in use; they only foreshadow what he may develop.

As always, blue stands for will or self-determination; the winglike bands of blue in the upper part of this child's aura indicate that this power was just beginning to unfold in him. It is reflected in the large patch of blue on the lower left, which results from his efforts to begin to exert some control over his environment. It also indicates a tendency to push himself beyond his capacity, which would drain his energy and reflect on his health.

As for his higher capacities, the purple represents an overshadowing spirituality, which, considering his other qualities, may develop into a genuine interest in the study and practice of spiritual ideals. The shade of green which can be seen in the upper part of the aura indicates sympathy, together with the kind of idealism which we see reflected in the pink. In this case it could develop into a concern for social problems and an active interest in human welfare and environmental reform.

The karmic indicators reveal that some of his troubles in life will come from his interactions with people he has to deal with. I realize that a statement of this kind may seem very general and almost commonplace, in that the problems of most human beings involve personal relationships. Since these indicators are very difficult to read, I can only repeat that they point to the primary areas where an individual's temperament and characteristics — or personal karma — may cause problems. In this case, there is an innate sensitivity which may make him vulnerable to hurt. There are also indications that his idealism is such that it may be difficult for him to put his ideas into practice in a way that satisfies him. His intense interest in many different subjects will be a source of great joy to him, but may also distract him sometimes from concentrating on the immediate work before him.

Fifty years after this painting was made, the subject is a man who still has a real feeling for language, and has developed great skill in communicating. Thoughtless or careless words irritate him, for he is very sensitive to shades of meaning. He has never had any difficulty in relating to people. As a child he spoke easily and was not shy, and in later life he has always been able to express his thoughts fluently and clearly.

He has had a number of years of successful teaching behind him, and has also worked extensively with computers and computer programming. His active and inquiring mind continues to engage his interest in many different fields. His commitment to spiritual principles, whose indications were present in him as a child, has grown in strength and depth, so that he tries consciously to live his life in a way that he feels is consonant with these truths.

5. An Adolescent Girl

At adolescence, the shape of the aura is approaching the oval form of an adult, but still remains more rounded at the top and bottom. This is the picture of a normal, healthy girl about fifteen years of age who was experiencing all the doubts and uncertainties which are common to this stage of life.

You will see that the green band which represents one's ability to put ideas and feelings into practice has now fully developed and extends to the edges of the aura. In her case, the band is fairly wide and somewhat dark in color, of a shade which indicates that she might have some artistic sensitivity. The blurred effect at the edges, as well as the wavy lines of pink, are due to the fact that she was as yet unable to distinguish between the things she did and the things she felt. At this time of life, dreams and yearnings are powerful, but still nebulous.

At the very bottom of her aura, the dark blue overcast with gray indicates her form of selfishness or self-centeredness, which made her dislike interference and want her own way—again, not an unusual characteristic of teenagers. It is really a manifestation of a developing will, a drive to assert oneself. In the case of this girl, the emotion is mixed with strain, since she felt that she was not succeeding in being herself, and this made her ill at ease. She did not mean to be selfish, but the strain often made her so. The brown and green just above this dark blue band represent the more ordinary kind of selfishness which wants things, pleasures and so on. The lines of blue extending into the pink just above show that the strained, uneasy feelings she experienced extended even into the things she liked to do.

The symbol of a horse's head covering her feet is very interesting. It reflects her tremendous love of horses, but its violet color shows that this feeling went much deeper than a young girl's usual fondness for riding, for it is a lower expression of the loftiest color in her aura. All her highest, even spiritual longings were in a sense precipitated into her feeling for horses, which symbolized her passion for freedom and for release from the difficulties and uncertainties of her life—difficulties, you understand, which were mostly in her own mind. However, at the time this picture was painted she was experiencing some friction at home, especially with her father, who tended to be quite domineering and set in his ways. The spirals on the left near the knees show a fairly long-lasting irritation with her parents.

The little scene which appears in her green band bears this out, for it might be described as a dream of action and of freedom. Whenever she was upset or unhappy, she would visualize herself on horseback, unfettered and free, galloping on and on through wild and open

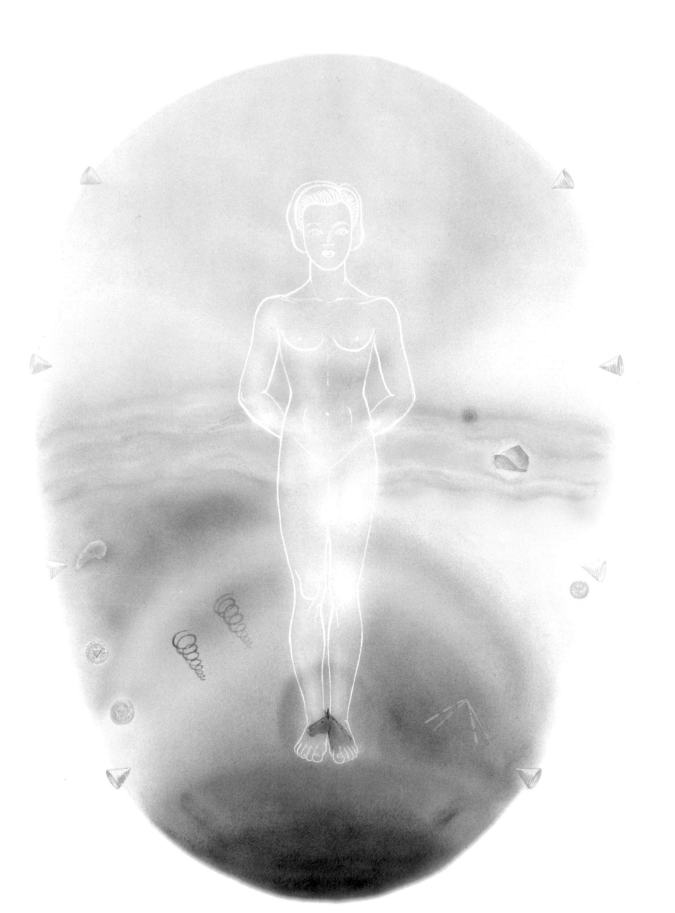

5. An Adolescent Girl

country with nothing and no one to hinder her. It is a symbol of revolt against her present circumstances — a symbol which is complemented by a sort of blue whirl, also in the green band, caused by her desire to do things and her frustration because she did not know how or where to begin.

She was really an affectionate girl, as you can see from the large area of pink in her aura, but even while going out to others she was apt to hold herself in check. Just now her emotions were all mixed up with the things she was thinking about, and this tended to confuse her. She was not completely alive to reality, for she still lived partly in a dream world. There is a good deal of yellow-green in her aura, which shows she had considerable capacity for both artistic and intellectual achievement if she could bring her faculties into balance, which was certainly not the case at the time. Just then her mind, which was essentially excellent, was to some extent blocked by her chaotic emotions.

All this is borne out by the yellow above the green band. The blue-green on the opposite side, whose color is reflected in her green band, shows her feeling for beauty, and again suggests she might have some potential artistic ability. The pale lavender-pink above is a mixture of affection and an aspiration for freedom and self-identity. The combination, in her, would probably take the form of a deep feeling for nature and for living things when she was older, and a generous desire to help people as much as she could.

You will note that her karmic indicators are smaller than those in the younger children, and that they have moved to the edges of her aura. Moreover, the shape has changed; the whirls are less compact, more unfolded, and their nuclei are open and almost triangular in shape. This is because much of their energy has already been absorbed into the aura. However, I could still perceive that although her affections would always be strong, her innate reticence would make it difficult for her to express them. There are also indications that she might be inhibited in some ways from fully realizing her innate capacities.

At this age, young people are very often a mixture of uncertainty and assertiveness, in revolt against their parents, wanting their own way, and not at all sure what that way might be. This aura, therefore, is of interest because it is fairly typical of the state of mental and emotional flux which characterizes adolescence.

I have not kept in touch with this girl through the years, but I have learned from her friends that although she broke with her parents upon her marriage, they became reconciled later in life, and she cared for her mother in old age. However, she and her parents were never really close, and she refused to accept their ideas or ideals as her own. Nor did she ever realize her dream of a life in which horses would play an important part. Nevertheless, her life was successful in that she did achieve her desire for independence. As a result, she became a well-adjusted and much happier person, with a good marriage and a pleasant family life.

Maturity

To illustrate the changes that take place in the aura when an individual reaches maturity, I have chosen two examples, a man and a woman, each of whom was at the time a well-balanced, active individual in the prime of life. You will see at once that the auras of adults are on the whole quite complex, since by the time one has become adult a variety of past experiences have left their mark, and often influenced the tenor of one's life.

Both of these individuals had certain talents and interests; both were busy pursuing their careers, as is normal at that time of life. Their experiences were very different, yet they had in common a characteristic which probably sets them apart from what we might call the ordinary man or woman in the street. While neither was religious in the strict sense of the word, in their different ways they were both idealists who aspired to put ethical principles to work in their lives. The results of these interests, however, show up differently in

their auras, since their lives, their characters and their karma were
entirely different.

6. An Artist in Her Thirties

The first thing we note is that this is a fully developed aura in which
all the characteristics described in Chapter IV are visible. Since this
is a person who was actively engaged in pursuing her career, the potentialities represented in the upper part of her aura are reflected in the
lower part, which expresses what she was doing and feeling at the
time. This symmetry is indicative of a well-balanced individual who
was using her abilities quite freely.

This is the aura of a practicing artist who had earned her living
for some years through the exercise of her talent. If I had not known
this to be the case, I should have perceived it at once because of the
width, shade and luminosity of her green band—all of which indicate that she was a skilled artist, with a good degree of coordination
between eye and hand, or perception and performance. She was, in
fact, earning her living in the field of applied arts, and had been doing so for some years, having worked successfully in a number of different media: she painted, but she also made stained glass, and she was
even a good carpenter. Thus she was both practical and versatile. All
this shows up in her green band, and in the fact that it extends lower
down in the aura than is usually the case.

The bottom of the aura is tinged with the brown of selfishness, or
self-centeredness. This is almost instinctual in human beings, since
it seems to be present in everybody in one form or another. Appear-
ing at the extreme bottom, as it does here, the selfishness is more a
kind of inherent or latent desire to be oneself, or to have the things
that make it possible to be oneself, rather than an egotistical desire
to be the center of one's world.

The lowest part of the aura contains the residue of our experience
in early life; that which lies below the feet has mostly passed out of
our consciousness but may affect us in unconscious ways. Even as a

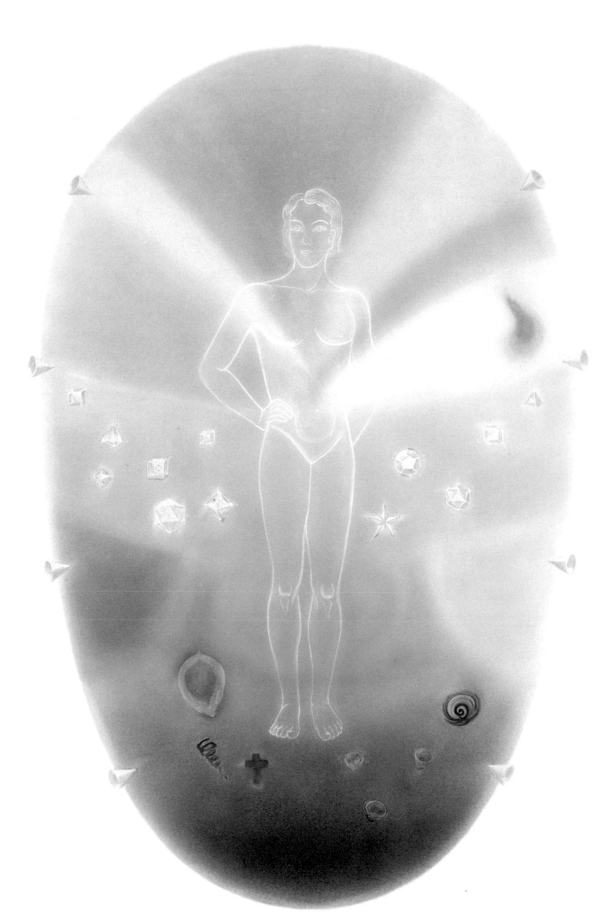

6. An Artist in Her Thirties

child, this woman experimented with different ways of doing things, as shown by the large area of green around her feet. When green is mixed with the brown, as it is here, this indicates confusion, born of the desire to express oneself in some way without knowing how to do it. (Something similar was seen in the adolescent girl.) The whirls at the bottom result from her childish yearnings, as she was apt to mull things over and over within herself. The blue cross is caused by her dreams as a child, which were often frightening, but also by her vague aspirations to realize and express the highest part of her nature.

The other yellow and green whirls, which are somewhat higher up in her aura, are reflections of experiences which she had during adolescence and early youth. Their colors indicate that she had undergone some worry and frustration in connection with what she wanted to do with her life. The red corkscrew shape must have been caused by an episode in which her affections were engaged, but it was painful to her and made her feel trapped. The drop-like formation on the left results from a more idealized affair of the heart which was pleasant rather than painful, and may not even have been a conscious involvement. When configurations like these appear somewhat higher in the aura, this shows that they were more recent, for as I have said, the lower part of the aura reflects time past as well as growth and present activity.

At the time the picture was painted, this young woman was concentrated on her art and on earning her living by this means. But she was also interested in metaphysical ideas, and in the relationship between art and ideal forms, such as those described by Plato. Thus she had a strong feeling for order and was also developing what might be called a symbolic turn of mind, which she was seeking to express. The yellow which appears in two places at the top of her aura indicates this intellectual search, as well as an aspiration to understand something of the laws of nature.

The figures within her green band reflect her interest in dynamic symmetry, which was somewhat in vogue at that period. She was trying to understand the geometric principles basic to form and structure, in both nature and art. These would not be a permanent feature of her aura, for as her attention and interest shifted to other things they would gradually fade away. At the moment she was completely focused on bringing her artistic training to bear on her work, and also on realizing in her artwork the principles of form which she found of so much interest.

The purple splash just below the green band is an unusual color to find in that part of the aura. It shows her efforts to bring her intuitive faculty into expression in physical life. The corresponding patch of yellow on the opposite side represents a similar effort to bring her mind to bear upon her physical experience, but the color is not quite so clear as the purple, showing that she had been less successful in this effort.

Another interesting configuration in this aura is the pink flame within the yellow which denotes her faculty of mind. It is caused by a feeling of admiration and respect for someone who had stimulated her intellectual interests, particularly in the study of archetypal forms. This, plus the juxtaposition of the pink and yellow with the blue-violet on the opposite side, shows that she liked to think, and also that she had a tremendous desire to be able to use her intuitional mind. The paleness of the color, however, shows that while she had the innate capacity, she was not exercising it very much at the time. The streaks of blue-green on one side, and blue on the other, relate to her perception of beauty as a high ideal, in the Platonic sense, and to her feelings of devotion to this ideal.

Although there is a good deal of pink in the upper part of the aura, which shows that she had an affectionate nature, this is not reflected so considerably below the green band. It seems that at that time she had no close personal relationships except with her brother and her mother.

Summing up my impressions, I felt that this was a person who should always enjoy good health, so well-balanced was her aura, and so free her expression on the physical plane.

Later in life this young woman moved to the West Coast, where she continued to earn her living in various artistic fields. Subsequently she had to give up her painting, for her mother became ill and entirely dependent upon her. Thus her personal karma prevented her from realizing all her hopes with respect to her art. She accepted this situation very courageously, and became increasingly close to her mother, so that her potential for warm and affectionate relationships did develop further. She never married, but lived quietly until she was in her eighties, enjoying good health, and retaining her balanced outlook and serene disposition.

7. A Man in His Forties

This is the portrait of a vigorous man in his prime, who was about forty-five years of age. His potentials were well-developed, and he was in the midst of an active life, with all its attendant difficulties and problems. This is indicated by the strong coloration of the aura, especially in the lower part. The darkness of the colors also signifies that he was a self-contained, reticent person who did not share his feelings with others easily. This was a man of strong character, and of powerful emotions which sometimes pulled him in different directions, for he had high ideals which he was determined to live by, and they created conflicts in him.

At the top of his aura, the large areas of blue indicate the potentiality of a deeply religious, devotional nature. Within this, the different shades of blue, particularly the one with a purple hue, show that he would always seek an ordered or ritualistic approach to spirituality; his ideal would be the kind of moral order which could create a world of perfect justice, reflecting spiritual principles and values.

The yellow above the green band shows that he was thoughtful and had a good mind, but he was not an intellectual. In his case, the yellow is merging into a yellow-green just below it, which in turn impinges upon his green band. All these juxtapositions show that he was consciously trying to develop more open, sympathetic relationships with people. The pink whirls in this yellow-green color result from

7. A Man in His Forties

his efforts to understand how he could apply what he was studying to his own life, as altruistic goals. These efforts were often tinged with annoyance. They are representative of the kind of mixed feelings so many of us experience, for it is quite possible to feel two diametrically different emotions at the same time. In his case, there was a combination of irritation with a genuine desire to do the best he could, and to be helpful to others.

His green band is not particularly wide, and its yellowish tinge indicates that physical work was not his metier. He was, in fact, not very clever with his hands, although he would have liked to have been. He occasionally tried to perform some task that required physical skill, such as a bit of carpentry, but without too much success. The patterns of yellow and pink which stretch throughout his green band are another reflection of his fundamental orientation toward order. They represent his work, which was methodical and regulatory, utilizing his natural tendency to think in a systematic way and to establish order and system in whatever he was doing. The fact that half these patterns are pink, rather than yellow, shows that he was trying to express affection and friendliness towards others. He was always eager to help the causes he supported, especially in organizational ways, which was where his talents lay.

Looking at the reflections of the past in the lower part of his aura, it is apparent that this man must have had a very difficult childhood, surrounded by people of strong, even violent, emotions. The sediment of reddish brown at the very bottom of his aura, which has an overlay of gray, shows the repercussions on him of strong feelings which boiled up around and even within him as a child, although he tried to resist them. Though the violence was not directed at him, he suffered from it, as children do. The small, tight whirls within this color are remnants of his early painful experiences, for the scenes that he witnessed were a shock to his nervous system and affected him deeply. The reddish brown color also indicates that in his youth he loved pleasure and luxury, and put a high value upon having the good things of life—an attitude which he had largely outgrown.

The snake-like form below his feet is not only a symbol of recurrent nightmares, but also an indication that some of the people close to him as a child were filled with hostility, and quarreled bitterly in his presence. The cross also indicates fear and conflict, but in this case such feelings were connected with his religious upbringing. These symbolic forms are low in the aura, below the feet, which means that they were related to his early life, but even so, they are marks which he continued to bear as an adult.

The bands of green and purplish red on the lower right side of the picture result from activities which aroused very strong feelings in him. In his youth he was quite rebellious, and he aligned himself with the revolutionary movement in Russia, which in those early days was filled with idealists who were charged with zeal for human betterment. The red bands show that he must have been associated with violent acts, but the fact that they alternate with bands of green indicates that his motivation was sympathy for human suffering, and that he believed he was helping people. As these bands reach quite high up in his aura, the emotions connected with them had not entirely disappeared; he still could be aroused to anger by what he perceived as social injustice.

The dark blue next to these bands is a religious feeling, which partly reflects the blue high up in his aura. It shows that in his youth he was searching for some kind of spiritual movement which he could feel was authentic, but that his search was half-hearted and without real conviction. It was only much later in his life that he found what he was looking for.

There is also blue on the opposite side of his aura, but of an entirely different color. The fact that it lies outside the pink of affection, at the edge of the aura, shows that he was inhibited in the expression of his feelings. He was really an affectionate man, and wanted to be kind and generous to those he loved, but he found it very difficult to be spontaneous and express his feelings openly.

The large orange plume seems to grow out of this color. You will see such formations in other auras, and they are always related to pride, self-confidence and self-esteem. This particular plume is somewhat loose and fluffy, which shows that he was not fixed in his conviction of being right, but that he had confidence in the ideas he had espoused and was determined to follow them. The position of this plume next to the blue and the pink indicates his perseverance in spite of the opposition of someone who was dear to him — in this case, his wife. The orange tint which impinges on the pink shows that although he was always fond of his wife, her criticism often sapped his self-esteem.

He had had a turbulent life with many traumatic experiences, and even now his life was not an easy one. The dashes within the patch of green just below the green band show his problems and difficulties in his business, and the fact that the dashes are pink connects these problems with his wife. Sadly, although she supported him in many ways, especially financially, she was never in sympathy with the things that mattered most to him.

The spiritual search which had been frustrated in his youth had brought him fairly recently into touch with an organization founded upon the ideal of the brotherhood of humanity. To him, this group seemed to embody all the high ideals which had impelled the revolutionary activities of his youth, and he joined it enthusiastically. For the rest of his life he remained a devoted member of this organization, and tried to model his life and conduct upon its ethical principles. Again, his wife did not share his interests or sympathize with his aspirations, although she did not directly interfere with his activities. Because he had a strong sense of loyalty to her, he had to believe all the more strongly in what he was doing. He imposed his code of conduct upon himself quite strictly, and he was somewhat rigid and set in his ways, but he was never intolerant of others. All of this is reflected in the orange plume in his aura, but the fact that it is loose in texture and not well-defined indicated to me that in later life, as he became more at ease with his new-found ideals, it would tend to dissipate and fade away.

This man was fundamentally a caring person, perhaps not so much loving as sympathetic. He liked people and was very kind and approachable, and as a result he had many friends who were fond of him. He loved children and delighted in being with them and sharing their interests, for unfortunately he never had any of his own. Perhaps because of this he was very fond of animals, and had a dog to which he was devoted.

This picture is especially interesting in that it shows an aura in transition, and reflects an individual's struggle for self-mastery. There is a lot of conflict, because this man was trying to reconcile his natural impulses and resolve his personal dilemmas in accordance with the spiritual ideals to which he had committed himself. When meditation was recommended to him he embraced the practice wholeheartedly, and because his temperament was methodical, he followed it regularly every day. The effect of this was beginning to create more balance and order in his aura; you can see reflections of his higher nature in the colors which represent his daily life, in spite of the temporary turbulence. This indicates not only that he was drawing upon his inherent potentialities, but also that his higher qualities were being reinforced and strengthened by his action and behavior.

Such was this man's dedication that at the time of his death, about twenty years later, I am sure his inner conflicts were largely resolved. I base this supposition upon the degree of brightness that was emerging in both the upper and lower portions of his aura.

8. Old Age: A Woman in Her Nineties

This is the aura of a woman who was ninety-two years old at the time I saw her, and the evidences of her advanced age are clearly visible.

First of all, the whole aura is covered with a filmy gray veil which is especially heavy over the lower part. It results from the clouding of her faculties, for she was no longer alert and did not remember things very well. Her activity in the world was much diminished, and lay mainly in the past. At the same time, her energy level (which is impossible to show in the picture) had slowed down measurably. Thus it is the past rather than the present which is revealed in her aura.

In marked contrast to the children, whose auras were dominated by their potentialities, the auras of the aged are often mainly a record of their past experiences and accomplishments.

Because of this, one might think that the colors of the upper part of the aura would be even more dimmed than the lower, but this is not the case. Her memories of the past had somewhat faded from her mind, and her emotions were no longer felt so strongly as before, but her higher principles were still active in her. Therefore the colors at the top of the aura remain bright and vivid. However, the yellow does not go to the edges of her aura, because she was not drawing upon her mental powers very much at the time.

Another condition which is caused by age can be seen at the edges of her aura. The boundary is blurred, for there is no sharp distinction between her own feelings and the general emotional field. This probably resulted from her lack of response to, and exchange with, her emotional environment at that time.

Looking at her aura, I had the impression that a strong will had always been the outstanding characteristic of this woman's personality. The gray-green which appears at the bottom of the aura indicates the form her selfishness must have taken — a determination to go ahead and do things her own way, come what may. She probably had enforced her will on other people to quite a considerable extent. In her early life she must have suffered a good deal of strain and depression, for there is a lot of gray low down in the aura. This probably was probably due to the strict upbringing which was customary in Victorian times, and which a young person of her temperament would have found very repressive.

The colors just above are also tinged with gray, which shows that somewhat later in life she went through a difficult period when she was thrown upon her own resources. She was born in 1847, when women were far from emancipated and had to struggle very hard to achieve anything for themselves. The gray whirls are the residue of worries which concerned her very much at the time, but they have faded and grown small, since it was all so long ago.

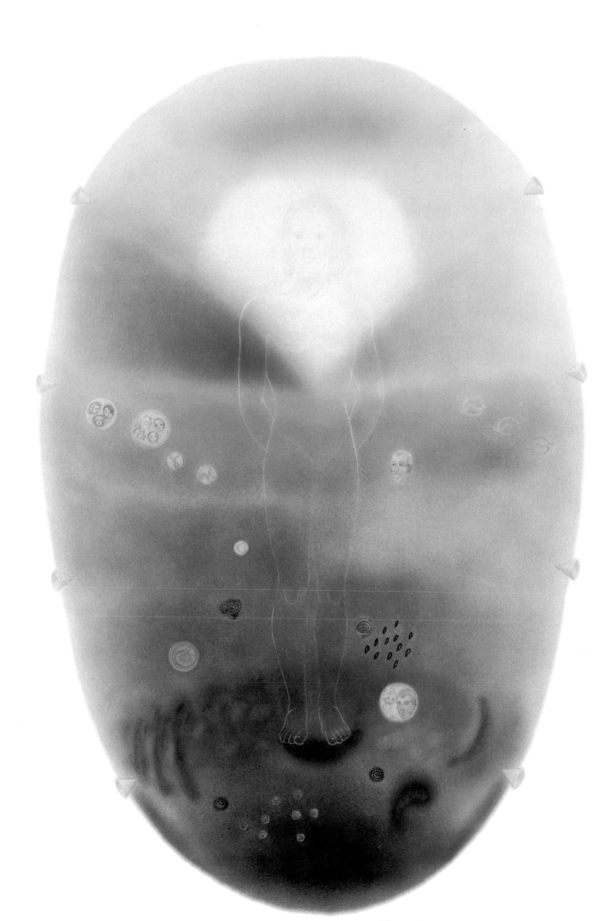

8. *A Woman in Her Nineties*

The pink in the upper part of her aura is very clear, and reveals her genuine feelings of kindness and affection, as well as her altruism. This pink is reflected below, but it is dimmed with age. She was married to the captain of a clipper ship in the China trade, and had three daughters and one son. Her husband died young, and perhaps it was because of this that she focused all her deepest affections upon her son. She adored him and he was very good to her, but he also died young, while his children were still small. His death was a blow from which she never entirely recovered, for the purple-blue with a gray whirl in it, which appears on the left side of the aura, is the remains of a period of deep sorrow in her middle life. There are other signs of past tragedies, such as the greens which lie low in the aura. These were now half-forgotten, but she was still not entirely free of them.

An interesting picture appears low down on the right side of her aura, for it is a composite portrait of her son both as a baby and as a grown man. The reason for this double image is that his memory became for her the symbol of childhood, and embodied for her the needs and rights of children everywhere. It was her deep love for her son that first aroused her interest in child welfare — an interest which grew into a lifelong concern, and led her into the fight for women's suffrage.

Her whole life was devoted to the cause of women and children, and she worked steadfastly for the reform of child labor laws and the abolition of slum conditions. This was not to her an academic interest; she was passionately and personally involved in the causes she espoused. Her work was always concerned with real individuals, not abstract issues. But since this work had ended more than twenty years before, and the people involved were long dead, all that had been most real to her had grown dim.

What remains is the impression of a strong character, grown even stronger by her life experiences. She was an idealist who spent her life's effort in translating her principles into social action. She had to fight for her values in a man's world, and achieve her independence at a time when few women succeeded in striking out for themselves. She was something of a pioneer in the field of social welfare, and was active in many movements dedicated to raising the standards of living for poor women, who had at the time few legal rights.

She was born into a wealthy family of good social position, but instead of making her complacent this caused her to feel she had to do something to help others less fortunate. As I said, her involvement was always with individuals, on whose behalf she was willing and eager to fight any opposition. Thus the faces which appear in her green band are at once reminiscent of those she fought for and a symbol of the personal concern she brought to her work.

During her long life she was very active and achieved many things. At the time I saw her she was a very old lady — a mere shadow of what she had once been. But all her past deeds, as well as the motivations and feelings which prompted them, were symbolized in her aura. It was therefore a record of her life.

VI
The Dedicated Life

The next group of portraits (four men and two women) is made up of very dissimilar people, whose lives and temperaments were so different that they might seem to have had little in common. There are two musicians, a painter, an architect, a social reformer and a young mother. But they share one very important characteristic: all of them were devoted to an art, an ideal, a cause which was basically the most important thing in their lives. Their orientation was therefore in the direction of something which transcended mere personal interest, no matter to what degree their personal lives might have been involved in its pursuit.

This does not mean that these people did not have the same kinds of problems which fall to the lot of most of us — problems involving human relationships, frustrations, losses and disappointments. They did, for often their purpose conflicted with their personal lives. This almost always produces signs of stress, which we will see in some of these auras. But their deep commitment to what they had chosen as their path gave their lives a direction which had its own authenticity. They could always find solace in their art or their ideas when events were troublesome, or when people became too intrusive. This abiding interest offered them a perspective into a larger world, an ideal realm which always maintained its integrity in spite of personal troubles, whose higher energies were able to refresh and renew their sense of purpose.

This kind of inner connection with what is perceived as our life purpose is present to some degree in many of us. We may think of it as associated with the arts, but scientists, teachers, priests, social workers, government servants, judges, environmentalists and many, many others are similarly motivated. In all such people, love of their work, or of the cause it furthers, transcends worldly gain, the need for security, or the desire for personal power and success.

Perhaps this kind of dedication is rarer today than it was when people had strong feelings of obligation to their family and to their country. Whatever the reason, lack of purpose can be a demoralizing influence, as I shall try to show in later chapters.

These six people all had a clear sense of direction in their lives, because they were committed to an ideal. They were also all strong characters in their different ways. Whether that inner strength caused or was caused by their commitment, I cannot say.

9. A Pianist/Composer

Our first subject is an elderly man who had been a world-famous pianist as well as a composer, although his compositions were never widely performed. At the time when this portrait was painted, he was slowly recovering from a stroke which had paralyzed his hands and arms, and severely curtailed his ability to play the piano. In spite of this, I have not included this man in the group of those affected by illness, because his mind and speech were not impaired, and he was making extraordinary efforts to overcome his disability. He had always been a fundamentally strong and healthy man who had succeeded in everything he attempted to achieve, and he was determined not to give in to his illness.

He was, however, suffering a great deal of stress. This is very evident in his aura, where the areas of blue and gray clearly show the signs of strain and painful effort. At the time I saw him, he would work every day with the therapist and then force himself to play the piano with his left hand, for the right was totally incapacitated. He made such an effort when I was with him because he thought it would give me pleasure, but it was really torture to watch.

The gray cloud in the middle of his aura, over the solar plexus, is caused by the reduction in his energy level, while the orange streaks within it are the result of injections which were being given him on a regular basis. A stroke of course affects the brain, but in his case his mind was clear, and therefore the effects of the illness do not show in the upper part of his aura. This is at least partly because he did not think of himself as ill or other than temporarily disabled.

But it was obvious to me that his severely strained condition had been long-standing and persistent. At the bottom of his aura, around the feet, there is a large area of mottled brown and green, which shows that from early childhood he had been made to work very hard indeed. He had been a child prodigy, and from his earliest years had been under great pressure from his family to perform well. As a matter of fact, his nervous system had never been free from tension.

Somewhat higher on the left side, around his feet, there is a lighter shade of green tinged with yellow, which not only testifies to the extraordinary amount of hard work he put in, but also to his efforts to think about and understand what he was working on. Everywhere in his aura you will see combinations of yellow and green, all of which show the degree to which he always applied his mind to the perfection of his art. But the colors and shapes below his feet show that when quite young he had experiences which both worried and frightened him. He must have been surrounded by people whose demands upon him arose out of their selfish interests, and the blue whirl and gray plume are the result of his somewhat oppressive sense of obligation, and his anxiety that he would not be able to please and satisfy them.

On the right side, the mixture of brown-green extends upward into the pink, a color which is reflected on the left above an area of blue shading into green/yellow. All this indicates that his affectionate nature had always been troubled by family relationships that caused him anxiety and worry.

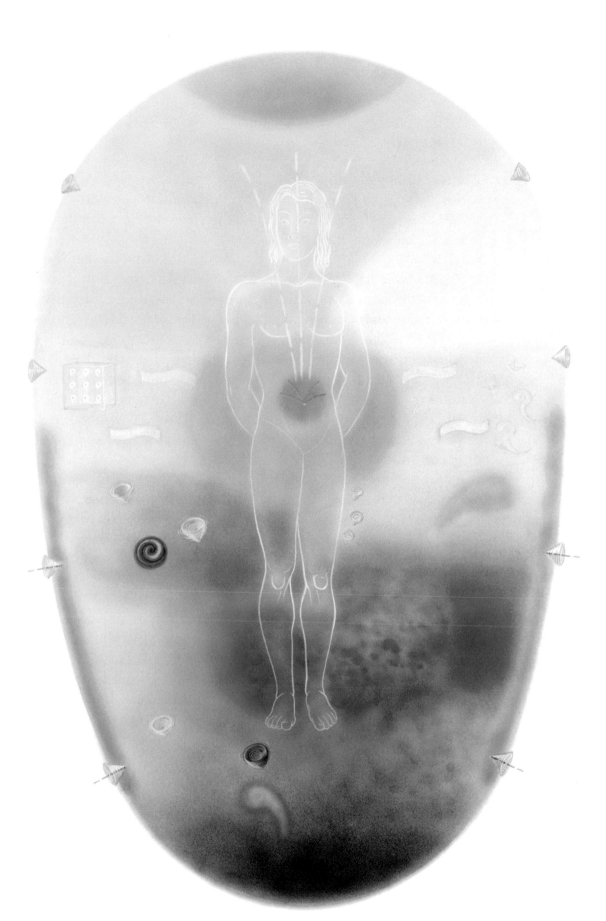

9. *A Pianist/Composer*

The continuous tension which he was under produced a sense of strain which began early in life and never abated. You will see blue lines at the edges of his aura, which reach down below the feet and extend into his green band. These lines are meant to suggest a condition which would be impossible to reproduce accurately, for in fact the whole lower part of his aura was overlaid with a film of blue. Such a condition (and you will see it repeated in other auras) always indicates persistent strain which has begun to affect the free flow of the energies of those emotions which are so constrained.

In this man's case, the stress was so severe that it had partially damaged the operation of the energy valves at the edges of his aura. The four lowest ones were leaking and sluggish, their movement being directly affected by the blue of strain which, as you will see, penetrates their centers. All this made him extremely nervous and kept his energy constantly below par, a condition which was of course aggravated by his illness. As I said, this was a very long-standing condition. I think that his family must have caused him endless trouble.

In contrast to the worry and strain revealed in the lower part of his aura, the upper part is clear, luminous and free. You will see a lot of pink in the lower aura, which shows that he was a kind man and affectionate in his relationships with family and friends. But there is no pink in the upper part of his aura, and this indicates that love was not one of his primary or most important characteristics.

In its place, there is on the left an area of green, which represents the quality of empathy or sympathy. It is from this aspect of his nature that his fundamental gentleness and kindness flowed. He did not feel passionately attached to people. He was altruistic, but not to the extent that he would have been led to sacrifice himself for others. Instead he exuded a general feeling of benevolence and good-will. He wanted to be helpful to people in whatever way he could. It is interesting that in a person who had been so much in the public eye there is no trace of the orange of pride and self-esteem. For such a famous man he had very little ego, and never thought of himself as too important to be of service to others.

At the top of his aura, above the head, there is a very large, vivid area of blue-green, which shows that his highest potential lay in his aesthetic perception—an intuitive feeling which enabled him to link his highest ideals (represented by the purple-lavender above) with his own aesthetic expression. The purple is touched with lemon yellow, which in actuality was so clear a color that it looked more like light shining through the blue-green. This fills the whole space above the head and reaches down to the green band in the middle of his aura—although this was temporarily obscured by the grayish cloud caused by his illness. Thus at the height of his powers his music was directly influenced by his deepest and purest insights.

The width of the green band, which extends from just below the heart to below the knees, also testifies to his ability to bring his musical ideas and sensibilities into physical reality through his playing. The color is a clear green-blue, which indicates his taste and discrimination, but it is also tinted with yellow, because he concentrated his mind so forcibly in his work. The yellow patterns and configurations in the green band are all symbolic, not only of his musical ideas but also of the meaning and significance he attached to them. The color of this band is brilliantly alive and shining at both sides, but dull and lifeless in the middle; this is the result of his illness, which was at that time inhibiting his ability to work almost completely.

There is a great deal of yellow in his aura, and indeed he was a highly intelligent man who brought his mind to bear upon everything he did. The green which appears in different parts of his aura, often mixed with yellow, comes from this propensity, and shows that his mind and his sensibility were freely expressed in his daily life. He had a thorough grasp of musical theory as well as of all the technical aspects of the piano, and the compositions he wrote, I am told, were very complex and difficult to play. His inquiring mind made him interested and curious about many things besides his own profession, which is somewhat unusual since musicians tend to be very engrossed in their art.

This is an interesting aura because it is so full of contradictions.

He had a great deal of artistic perception, as well as the ability to focus his mind and concentrate upon the solution of difficult problems, yet his emotions were strong and his personal relationships had long been in conflict with his ideals. Because he was very intelligent, he was fully aware of this conflict, and it caused him great concern. He had worried about his work and his family and his financial responsibilities for so long that it had finally become an emotional habit — a habit which marred his natural joy in his music, and undoubtedly contributed not only to his stroke but also to some recent symptoms of heart disease.

Although his temperament was naturally cheerful and outgoing, the friction within his family inevitably had its effect on him. I think some members of his family caused him endless trouble through their selfishness. They expected him to provide them with financial support, and made demands upon him which he gave in to out of a desire to escape their bickering and constant complaints. In addition, he was a man who had been accustomed to a full, active life and a successful career, so the restrictions imposed on him by his illness were galling, and made him very impatient. This aggravated his strain. But in spite of all these problems, he retained his natural sweetness and his sympathetic disposition.

This man's life was full of accomplishment, yet far from easy. His aura is a record of his past and present struggles, but above all it reveals a man who had been able to fulfill his early promise, and realize his highest talents and abilities to a remarkable degree.

10. A Concert Pianist

In marked contrast to the previous case, this man, although also a pianist, was of an entirely different temperament. In both cases, music was an absorbing passion, but while #9 had a curious, inquiring mind and was interested in many different things, this man lived and breathed only for his music. Moreover, #9 had had a stormy personal life, whereas the home environment of this man was sheltered and

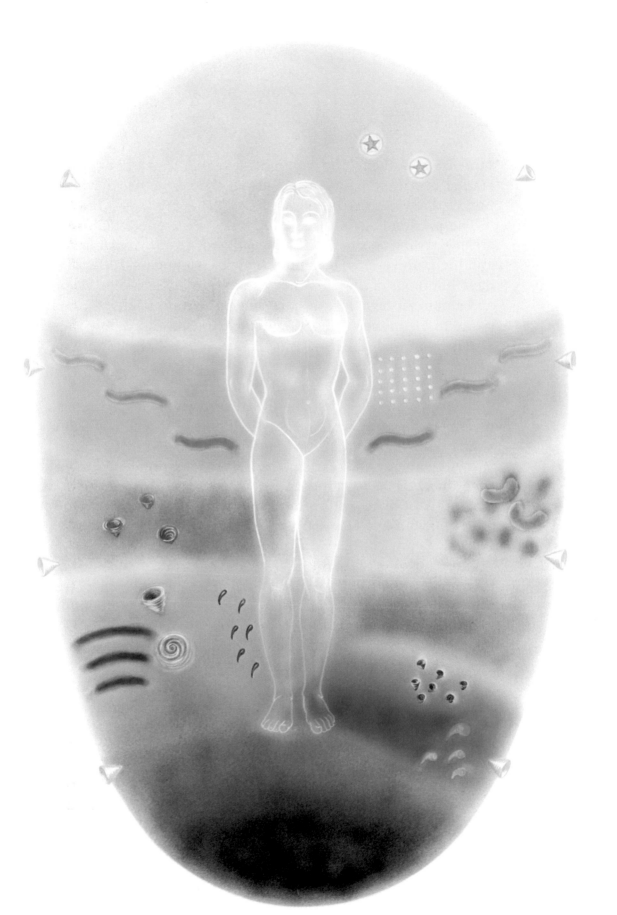

10. A Concert Pianist

supportive. Although he was in his seventies at the time, and his intake of energy was somewhat slowed down, he was quite healthy. For all these reasons, his aura is remarkably clear and free of stress.

The outstanding feature of this aura is the enormous amount of green, in varying shades. His green band, again, is extremely wide and high, and a most beautiful shade of sea-green — the lightest and most luminous of any of our cases. Within it are several wavy lines and a number of yellow dots, all ranged symmetrically. These forms relate to his music, which dominated his life; the yellow shows his absorption, and the blue the concentration of his will on his performance.

At the bottom of his aura, the mottled gray-blue does not extend very far upward, showing that these emotions lay far in the past, and no longer affected him. The gray indicates that when he was a very young child he found his surroundings somewhat intimidating, and was often uneasy and fearful. The blue results from his feeling at that time that he had to gather himself together and concentrate on his studies. All this related to a period of his life when he was around nine years old and was sent away from home all by himself to study music.

Just above, on the right, there is an area of dark blue-green, with four small plumes in it, as well as a number of small red whirls. The plumes result from the fact that when he was quite young he was pleased with himself and felt he was doing well, while the whirls are remnants of an emotion of almost righteous indignation which he had had at about the same time, and which he had not entirely forgotten.

Just below the green band, you will see on the left a cloud of rosy purple, which is balanced on the right by green, with some pink shapes within it. All of this relates to his music. The green shows the amount of work he still put into his playing, while the rose and purple reflect his feelings about his music, which were really a deep love and even reverence. This reverence was associated with the awe he felt for his teacher when he was a young man. He studied with Liszt, who was an overpowering personality as well as a consummate artist with an enormous technique, and the experience of this association always remained very vivid in his memory.

Lower down, on the left side, there are three blue bands as well as two fair-sized gray whirls and a number of reddish dashes. These all relate to a period in his life during which he was under a lot of stress, and which depressed him and at the same time made him very angry. He was born in Russia and had made his whole career in his own country, where he was very well known, but he was forced to leave at the time of the Revolution. He was separated from some of the members of his family and worried because he had no news of them. They were safely reunited in the United States, but these memories left their scars, and he could always be roused to indignation when reminded of the changes wrought in the Soviet Union.

Above the green band, the position on the right side, opposite the pink of affection, is where one usually sees the yellow related to the mind. In this case, however, that color is replaced by a pale green tinged with yellow — a clear shade, but cloudy in formation. This color expresses the feelings of sympathy and empathy which were his natural response to other people. Above this, the whole top of the aura is filled with shades of blue-green, signifying that his highest powers and sensitivities were related to art and its expression.

The most interesting features of this aura are the two bright golden stars placed high in this blue-green. The absence of a large amount of yellow shows that he had little interest in abstract ideas, and also that his work did not require him to use his concrete mind in practical ways. All this was replaced in him by a kind of intuitive insight (represented by the golden stars) which gave him the ability to understand musical ideas and solve musical problems almost without thinking. He had the unique ability to translate his artistic insights directly into his playing; his intuition and his hands worked together in harmony without any need for the mediation of the mind. This phenomenon was unique in my experience.

This man is an example of the dedicated life par excellence; for him, music was his whole life, his love, his abiding interest. As the clarity of his aura shows, his personality was simple and childlike, and he was so one-pointed that the colors are few and well-integrated. He had a very rigorous and intensive musical education in St. Petersburg before the Revolution, where he became friends with many of the famous composers active in Russia at that time. He himself had had a successful career, both as a pianist and as a conductor, but all this ended with the Revolution. After coming to the United States he gave a few concerts, but devoted himself mainly to teaching and editing piano scores.

Interestingly enough, the curtailment of his public performances did not make him at all bitter. He still had his music, he did not want financially and he had the full support of his family, all of whom adored him. His daughters were almost too caring, for they vied for his attention and were inclined to quarrel with each other over small indulgences. This affected him very little, however, for the whole family was united in the effort to give him the peace and quiet his music demanded. In contrast to #9, his home environment was completely protective.

This was a greatly gifted man. He had worked all his life in the service of his art, and as a result his personality had refined itself to such a degree that it became a clear instrument for the expression of his artistic insight. Because his personal life never interfered with his dedication to music, the troublesome events and difficulties he had encountered in the past had no power to destroy his basic serenity. One might say that here was a man whose karma allowed him to fulfill his highest aspirations.

11. A Social/Environmental Activist

Here, again, is the aura of a person who was devoted to an abstract ideal, but in this case, the ideal was one of social justice. Because of this man's temperament, the ideal became translated into a cause to which he was so totally committed that he was willing to sacrifice his whole career and even his personal security.

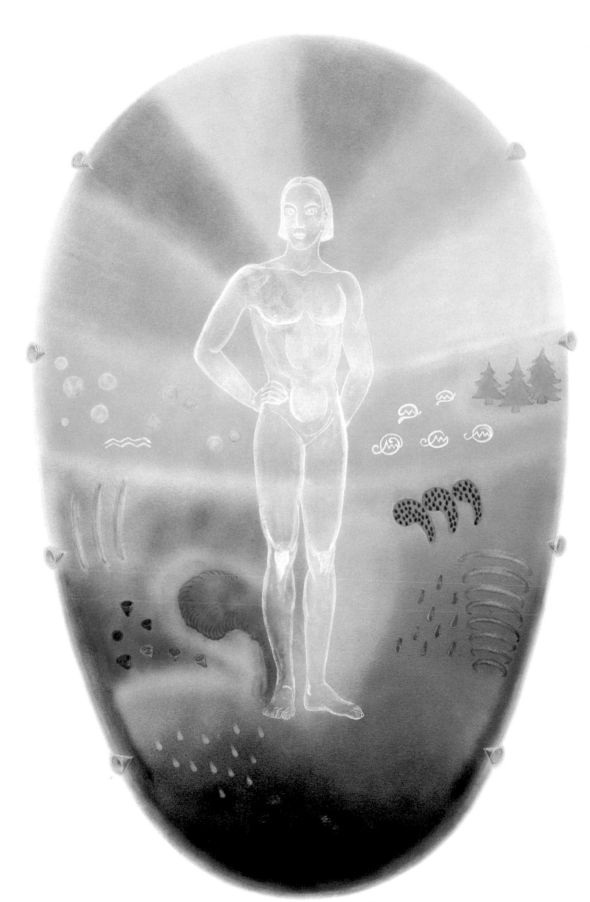

11. A Social/Environmental Activist

First of all, we can see from both the clarity and depth of the colors in his aura that this man — who was then in his fifties — was a person of very strong character. On the whole this is a well-balanced aura. Most of the colors at the top are brightened and amplified by their reflection in the lower part, for by his active use of his abilities he was increasing their strength and their energies. The broad band of golden yellow on the right shows by its width and brilliance not only that he had a fine intellect but also that he was constantly applying it to his work and to the implementation of his ideals.

This last is indicated by the proximity of the broad streak of green just above the yellow; the empathy and compassionate concern for others which the green represents touches and influences his thought. The shade of the large band of pink on the opposite side, which always indicates affection, reflects a genuine altruism — a strong feeling of concern for people, for humanity as a whole. The fact that this color is reflected in the lower aura indicates that in daily life he was a kind man, and friendly in his relationships. But at the same time, his affections were not very outgoing; the blue bars across the pink show that he kept them to himself and was even apt to repress them.

Purple or lavender above the head always stands for spirituality or for spiritual aspiration, as distinct from religious devotion, which is a different shade of blue. In this man's case, he was not religious and had little or no interest in theological or ontological concepts. To hear him talk, one would have thought him a thorough materialist, because he was so passionately dedicated to changing the world through social reform. But he was in fact an idealist whose essential spirituality took the form of commitment to the good of humanity.

The green band is wide and shows his practicality. He was not just a theorist, but spent his energies on trying to work out ways to put his ideas into action. He was a fine organizer, as well as a concise, fluent speaker and writer. He was also not afraid of using his hands, and loved such things as building houses and chopping wood and working in the garden. The symbols in the band indicate that he was very much preoccupied with the global economy and with social justice, but also that he had a long-term interest in environmental issues. These ideas were basic not only to his work but to his over-arching world view. As I have said, the forms within the green band reflect a person's fundamental concerns; his are related to concepts, and are therefore yellow. Such symbolic forms are usually quite long-lasting.

A more unusual pattern in the green band is the group of dark green trees. When I saw these, I asked if trees were a symbol of peace and harmony to him. He told me then that for many years before going to sleep at night he would visualize a certain group of trees in a spot he knew and loved, and that this seemed to put his day's work into a larger perspective; it gave him a sense of the peace within nature — a peace that endures in spite of turbulence and conflict. Later in life, when he turned his energies more in the direction of ecological issues, I am sure this symbol was an even greater source of inspiration to him.

One of the distinctive features of this aura is the amount of blue both above and below the green band. This indicates that he had a highly developed will, which he exercised freely in his daily life, especially on himself; he was often quite hard on himself. The plumes dashed with red which appear in the blue just below the band show that his reformist zeal was to a considerable extent fueled by anger; he took an adversarial stance because he expected people to oppose him. He not only spoke up for social changes; he got out into the arena and battled for them.

He had a great deal of self-control, but the pressures upon him resulted in considerable strain, which shows in the blue bands encasing the lower part of the aura. Remember that these bands are not just at the edges of the aura but surround it, covering but not obscuring the other colors. (You have seen a similar shell in #9.) They always indicate both nervous and emotional stress, and when they rise higher in the aura they can signal severe disturbance and even lead to physical disabilities, as in #17, because they block the free flow of emotional energy. But in this case I felt that the condition would be temporary, for this was an extremely strong and robust man, with a great deal of physical resilience.

This strain is related to the bottom of the aura, where the dark colors indicate that in childhood he probably lived in a somewhat repressed environment, and that he was strong-willed and defiant. Here, as always, there is a residue from the past, from emotions that one has largely outgrown but which still linger to some extent within the unconscious mind. In this man's case, it shows that as a child he was affectionate but shy and undemonstrative, as well as rather withdrawn into himself. The brown tinged with green shows the usual selfishness, and also that he was determined to have his own way. The greenish color relates to the fact that he did a good deal of hard manual work in his youth. The pink and blue vortices on the left are a sign that he had a good many difficulties in his relations with his family. Since they rise up fairly high in the aura, they must have lasted through his early adult life; on the opposite side, the dashes in the blue similarly represent surges of strong feeling. All these formations were temporary, and would eventually pass away.

Another interesting feature of this aura is the bright orange plume on the left side, close in to the body below the knees. You have seen a similar formation in #7, and there is another in #13. Their position, close to the body or farther out into the aura, indicate their degree of activity. As I mentioned in the earlier case, they are usually created by a strong conviction that one is right, and a determination to stand by that conviction no matter what the consequences may be. In a certain sense, therefore, such a plume represents intellectual pride. This man had it so strongly that he was sometimes contemptuous of those who disagreed with him. There is always the danger that those who hold powerful convictions may develop a form of self-righteousness and intolerance of those who oppose them. But as I mentioned in Chapter I, when this man saw a picture of the plume he recognized it for what it was, and made up his mind to change it. Such was his strength of will that he probably succeeded in doing so.

I have frequently been asked whether such intellectual pride stems from egotism. The conviction that one is right requires self-confidence, and usually there is some degree of egotism involved. But it is possible to have a strong ego and still be an altruist. This man was convinced that he knew how to achieve the goal of social justice (in which he was probably over-optimistic), but he was not self-seeking. He did not work for his own glory. Quite the contrary, he made a number of personal sacrifices in pursuit of his goals.

Early in life he became concerned about the social evils which he perceived in the United States in the days just after World War I, for at that time there were no child labor laws, and working conditions were deplorable. He determined to take a firm public stand on these issues, and began to spend most of his time in an effort to win legislation that would correct this evil. He was a well-known university professor, but his strongly voiced criticism of public policy met with a great deal of opposition both from colleagues and from the establishment, and as a result he lost his teaching appointment amidst a blaze of publicity. His radicalism brought him all kinds of accusations of disloyalty, and his views were considered by many conservatives to be subversive. He suffered personally from all this, but he never stopped speaking out for what he considered to be the truth, whenever and wherever he could find a forum.

In his later life (for he lived to be almost 100 years old), he turned his attention from political to ecological issues. He had always had a great love of nature, and as he grew older and the world picture changed so significantly, he began to turn his attention to practical ways of living simply and harmoniously with the environment. He developed many theories about growing and preparing food organically, and wrote several books with his wife on how to live harmlessly, using the Earth's resources without exploitation. He became as famous for his advocacy of this cause as he had been notorious for his early radicalism, and many people made pilgrimages to sit at his feet and imbibe the simple wisdom and goodness he displayed in his personal life.

This man was an idealist, and strong ideals stand the test of time. I said earlier that some of the colors in an aura embody the qualities of higher states of consciousness, and that these can come through to energize and enhance a person's ability to be effective in the world. Reflections of these levels may be seen in this man; in his case they are colored by sympathy and a deep concern for human suffering.

Fifty years after this picture was painted, I can say that this man succeeded in fulfilling his inner promise. Although I did not see him in the years before his death, I am sure that most of the complexities in this aura would have disappeared, because the irritations and frustrations of his early life would have long since been worked out. Moreover, there would be no strain, and a much more relaxed attitude toward life. Thus in later years his aura would have been much clearer and less complicated.

When the orange plume disappeared from his aura, the strong convictions it represented were replaced by a flowering of his innate love of nature. His efforts to find practical ways to nurture the earth, during his later life, were thus a fulfillment of tendencies glimpsed in his earlier years.

12. A Painter

When I first looked at this aura, even if I had known nothing about the person's history I should have been struck by the width of the green band, and by the preponderance of green elsewhere in the aura. Green and pink are the dominant colors. It is obvious that this was a person with warm, affectionate feelings, whose hands and mind worked very well together.

The unusual color as well as the width of the green band show that this woman's work was at once creative, skillful, and uniquely expressive of her artistic ideas. She was in fact a well-known painter. But she also had a high degree of manual dexterity, for she was a good carpenter and had been able to teach herself many practical skills.

Her aura is very interesting in a number of other ways, especially in what it reveals of her past life and the ways her experiences have continued to influence her.

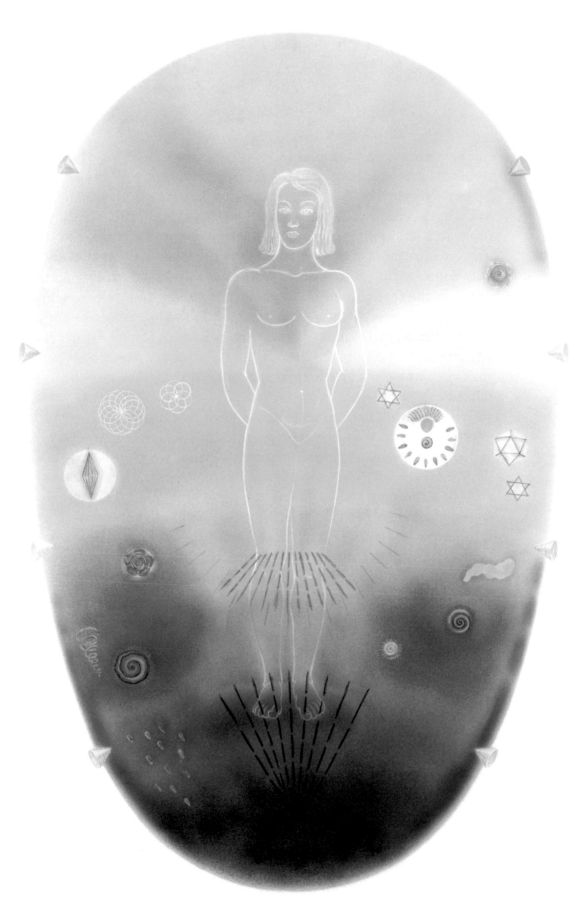

12. *A Painter*

The mixture of dark blues and greens at the bottom of her aura show that in childhood and adolescence she was severely repressed by her parents. Far from accepting this, she was fiercely rebellious, and often at odds with her family. The fact that these dark colors rise up to her ankles shows that in her early twenties she tried to break away from this environment without much success. As a result she was oppressed by a feeling of hopelessness and futility. Her spirit of revolt in the face of continual opposition put her in a state of chronic irritation, shown by the red dashes low on the left side. She showed artistic talent early in childhood, and made continued efforts to express herself through her painting, but her family situation was such that the future seemed hopeless to her, so that she was often very depressed.

The radiating lines of blue around her feet are indications of her youthful revolt, and her passionate desire to be herself. They are reflected in a similar pattern around her knees, which relates to a later period in her life. She was always fiercely independent, and when she felt circumscribed by others she reacted strongly. The break between these two patterns is due to the fact that there was a period in her youth when she was more accepting of the world she found herself in, and was therefore less strained and rebellious.

She grew up in England around the time of World War I, when social lines were firmly drawn and one did not move easily out of one's class. Her aristocratic family was extremely conservative, and had strict ideas about what a young girl should and should not do. She displayed artistic talent at an early age, and since it was both traditional and socially acceptable for young girls of good family to paint, she was given careful training. But she did not want merely to dabble at art; she made up her mind while she was still very young that she was going to be a painter and that art would be her life's work. This was not compatible with her conventional surroundings at a time when young girls were supposed to be both decorative and decorous. Thus she was constantly in a state of war with her family, who did everything they could to suppress what they considered her bohemian impulses. As a consequence, her feelings of rebellion and frustration grew day by day.

Her unhappiness was intensified by the fact that she suffered from a serious physical affliction. She had been born with impaired hearing, and while she was still young she became almost entirely deaf. In consequence, communication with others required a continuous effort, and created a great deal of the strain that can be seen at the bottom of her aura. This handicap affected her whole life, for it was always very difficult for her to carry on a normal conversation. When she came to sit for her portrait she carried a huge ear trumpet, which she would thrust out for me to shout into. I must say it made communication somewhat heavy going.

The misty gray in the lower aura resulted from her efforts during her late adolescence to break away from the repressive influence of her home environment. She longed to lead a creative life, but she was very unsure of her own ability and often felt gloomy about the future. Her self-doubt made her insecure and depressed. All in all, it was a very painful period in her life.

But just above the dark colors at the bottom of her aura, and in strong contrast, you will see a patch of rosy pink on the left, balanced by a violet-pink on the other side. These both rise up to her green band, and although the lines of strain at the edges of her aura persist, the upper parts of these two colors are free of any constraint. The reason for this marked change is that long ago she had had the good fortune to become close friends with a person who had great creative gifts, and who was also a forceful and vivid personality. This man took an interest in her and encouraged her to strike out for herself, both artistically and personally. He became her guide and mentor, and his influence literally transformed her life, for he encouraged her to break her connection with her family, leave home and move to the far West of the United States. She felt he took her out of prison into a new life of freedom, and her gratitude to him knew no bounds.

She idealized this man to such an extent that he continued to exert a tremendous influence over her even at the time the picture was painted, although he had been dead for a number of years. You will see two symbols in her aura which are mirror images of each other — one in the upper aura just at the juncture of the green and yellow, the other below, in the pink. These symbolic forms reveal her deep feelings about this person, whose memory still continued to inspire her. The upper symbol exerted a powerful spiritual influence over her artistic work, while the lower one energized her interactions with people. These show that the memory of this man still engendered an almost religious awe in her. She idealized him. Their relationship was entirely Platonic, for he was happily married, but perhaps because of the strength of her feeling for him she never married or had a love affair.

Although she had many warm friends and was very sympathetic, there was always some strain in the expression of her feelings, probably due to her deafness. This is shown by the blue bar at the edge of the green of sympathy in her upper aura. But there is a great deal of rose-pink, which is a sign that her affections were both warm and unselfish. The blue is her will, while the blue-green indicates the highest reaches of her artistic sensibility — her intuitive response to the aesthetic component of nature and of the world. The fact that this color touches her green band shows that she was trying to express this ideal in her own painting.

The symbols in her green band are much larger and more well-defined than usual, perhaps because, being an artist, she visualized clearly. The flame-like form within the circle is interesting because it symbolized to her the spiritual influence in art. When I described the symbol to her, she said that it accurately portrayed a vision that she had had in the desert — a vision that continued to be a source of inspiration to her. Although this experience had been totally subjective, she had made a painting of it which she later showed me, and which was indeed the symbol I had perceived, though much more beautiful and elaborate. Thus it remained very clear in her aura.

The other, larger symbol is connected with a painting she was working on at the time. She had been attending a series of concerts and drawing sketches of the conductor's hands in motion; this symbol represented her present interest in this study, and would have probably disappeared as she turned to other subjects. It is also interesting that the form this study took vaguely resembled the designs which Native Americans use in their arts. She herself had grown to feel very close to the Indian peoples, and was trying to understand the spirit of their culture in order to be able to represent them sympathetically as well as authentically in her painting. This interest unconsciously influenced what she was working on.

This aura is fascinating because there is such contrast between the past and the present. It is hard to imagine a life in which there could have been more radical change, for she exchanged a narrow, conventional environment for one of unrestricted freedom, and a life of wealth and luxury for one that was extremely simple, even Spartan. In later life she never thought about the conventions and was careless of her personal appearance, although always fastidious in her habits. She lived very plainly, with few possessions, and succeeded in immersing herself completely in a culture that was totally alien to her upbringing.

She had a deep love for the mountains and the Indian pueblos and the colors of the bare rocks and the sight of horses running on the open plains. In this environment she became herself at last; it was as though she had been reborn. When she was free to live the kind of life she deeply needed, she became more unified, less complex, and her own inner integrity began to shine through her work. This transformed her art, for when she was free to represent her own self, as well as her artistic insights, her painting came into its own.

13. A Designer/Architect

This is the aura of a man in his middle sixties who had trained as an architect but spent most of his professional life as a theatrical designer. He had a great love of drama and the stage, and many of his friends and associates were in the theatre. At the time this picture was painted, however, he had recently retired from his active work, and his greatest achievements were behind him. Although he still devoted a good deal of his time to writing, his major works had been published earlier. In other words, his peaks of achievement lay behind him, and he was in what one might call the reflective or contemplative period of his life.

This aura is remarkably clear and free from scars or stress, unlike those of #7 and #11, whose signs of early conflicts are still visible. When he was younger and more active this characteristic might not have been quite so evident, but his nature was such that I believe he would usually have been able to remain calm and serene. For this man had a remarkable degree of integration between his mind and his emotions. He had known from early youth what he wanted to be and to do; he had accepted certain philosophical, mathematical and spiritual ideas as guiding principles in his life and work, and he never found any reason to change them. This interest influenced his thought and shaped his life work. Since he had adopted a profession which lent itself to the expression of these ideas, he was never frustrated or inhibited, and this always makes for emotional health. His early life was, in fact, a total contrast to that of #12.

The cloudy gray-blue at the bottom of his aura indicates his form of selfishness, which was more a desire for self-expression and the opportunity to have his own way than an attachment to possessions. The dark green just above shows that he was very active when he was young, and ambitious as well. The color grows lighter on his left side, and it merges with a dark blue ring formation. The shape of this ring indicates that it is related to a memory which lies in the past but still influences him, while its proximity to an area of lighter, more brilliant blue, shows that the experience was a beautiful one, and painful only because it ended. In point of fact, this memory was inspired by a wonderful marriage to a woman who exerted a long-lasting influence upon him — an influence which he himself felt was of spiritual importance. Although she had died many years before, her memory was still a presence in his life, and he had never felt any inclination to remarry.

13. A Designer/Architect

Out of this patch of blue, which is a reflection of his higher will and sense of self, there rises an orange plume, much like those we have seen in the two auras referred to above. As always, this formation signifies a sense of pride and self-esteem; in this case, he was somewhat complacent about the fact that he knew so well what he was about. He was confident in the rightness of his ideas, as well as in his ability to embody them in his design work and expound them in his writing.

The blue-green on the lower right side is a sign that his artistic sensibility was very active in his daily life, an intrinsic part of whatever he was doing. On the opposite side there is an area of pink, which always expresses affection. As you can see, it touches the blue related to his early marriage, for his feeling for his wife had not disappeared. He was affectionate with his children and one or two intimate friends, but he had few personal attachments. On the whole there is not a great deal of pink in this man's aura. He was, as a matter of fact, a fairly aloof, very self-sufficient person, kindly, but not close to many people.

Looking at the upper part of his aura, one sees the presence of a fine intellect. The brilliance of the yellow shows that his mind was very active, and the fact that the color is reflected below the green band indicates that he used his mind to control his actions. The blue-green on the opposite side relates to his perception of beauty, and the lighter green plumes within it result from his feelings of sympathy with others who are similarly influenced. The bands of violet above the head show his deep, almost ritualistic feeling for what he thinks of as the spiritual principles underlying nature.

Within the wide green band you will see a whole array of intricate geometric forms. These figures are expressions of his constant preoccupation with the principles of form, which he felt reveal the underlying archetypal order in the universe. These symbols played an active role in his imagination and were woven into everything he did. They were so ever-present in his mind that no matter what he might have been doing, whenever he happened to have a piece of paper in front of him he would begin to sketch some of these intricate shapes. All his life he had pursued the study of the hidden mathematical principles which confer their harmony, symmetry and proportion upon the profusion of natural forms, and he had written several books on what was at that time known as dynamic symmetry, a study of the way in which forms derive from one another.

This was a man, I felt, who was born under a lucky star. His life had been singularly free of dissension, and if he had had worries, he had left them far behind. Although he had lost his wife, his memories of her were a source of happiness and comfort to him. He had been fortunate in pursuing a profession which he enjoyed, and in which he was very successful. While still young he had found a philosophy which was entirely satisfying and endlessly fascinating to him, and which he was able to put into practice in his life. His books were well received, if not widely popular. It is true that he lived a solitary life, but with this he was well content. He had in fact reached the state of serenity and detachment which, according to Hinduism, is supposed to mark the last period of life.

What makes this aura unique is that his mind was working in full harmony with his feelings. There never seems to have been a block between the two. His spiritual aspirations were tied to his love of beauty and to what he thought of as the divine order within the universe; both were to him expressions of an underlying spiritual reality. These ideas were the subject of his meditations as well as the constant preoccupation of his thought, and they brought his intuitive level of consciousness into harmony with his mind and emotions. Thus the three levels were working synchronously in him, which is a rarity.

14. A Youthful Idealist

I complete this group of portraits with a person who was quite different from the achievers who have gone before. In the first place, she was young (only twenty-five), with her life before her and no record of accomplishment behind. Thus her past experience had not shaped her character to any great extent. Nor did she have the talents which led most of the others to devote their lives to their artistic work. What she had in common with them was an overriding sense of purpose. In her case it became an almost passionate commitment to what she thought of as the goal of human life: the achievement of spiritual insight and values.

The whole thrust of this book has been towards the idea that individuals can take their lives into their own hands, put their intentions into practice, and make their aspirations a force for personal change. As I will try to show in Chapter VIII, I believe that motivation is the first requisite for change, and that one must have a clear sense of the direction in which one wants to go — of the path one wishes to follow, even if the end of that path is unknown or even unknowable. This girl found the direction she wanted to take when she was quite young, and she remained faithful in her determination to follow it all the rest of her life.

This commitment shows itself most strikingly in the wing-like bands of strong blue which rise from the region of her heart to the upper reaches of her aura. She had been practicing meditation for about four or five years, and these bands of blue are the result. They have to do with the unfolding of the will, and with her conscious effort to regulate her life in accordance with her spiritual ideals and to suppress her selfish impulses. Of all our cases, only this girl and #13 had this kind of dedication.

Interestingly enough, she was not a person one would ordinarily think of as strong-willed. She did not have the type of determination that forges a career in spite of handicaps, or develops a talent through sheer persistence. Like many teenagers, she had vacillated about what she wanted to do in life, and even at twenty-five she was rather indifferent about the kind of work she did, and tended to accept what was offered her. Thus she was not ambitious in the ordinary sense of the word. Nor did she desire to have control over anyone else's life. It was herself that she desired to control.

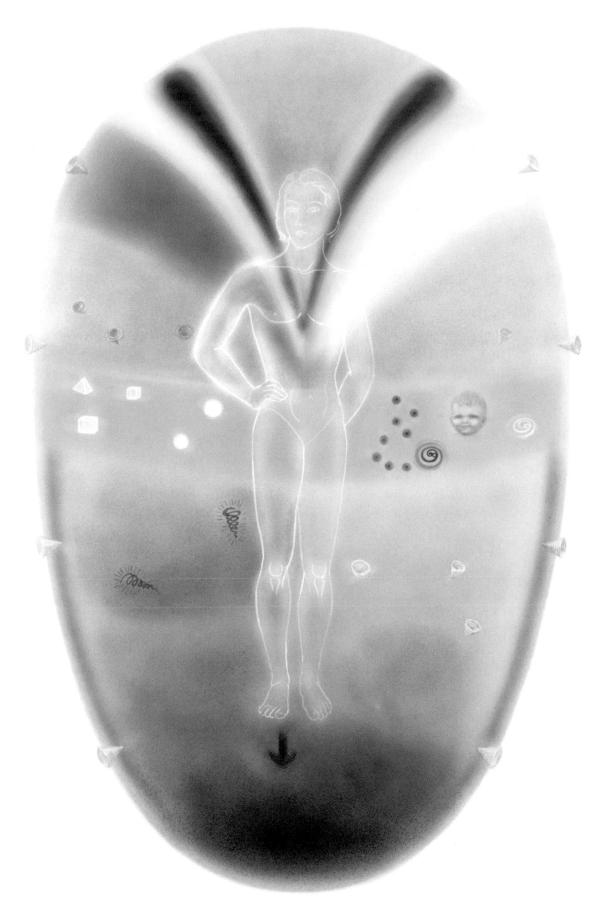

14. A Youthful Idealist

At this particular time, she had all the intensity of youth, and because her natural temperament was high-strung, she was very tense. She was a bit of a perfectionist, and was very impatient and critical, especially of herself. If she did not perform up to her standards she felt very badly about it. She put a great deal of pressure upon herself without knowing it, and as a result she was overstrained.

Because of her youth, the colors of her aura are clear, and there are few signs of trauma in her past. At the bottom of the aura, the dull gray-green shows that her basic selfishness took the form of a desire to express herself, rather than a craving for material things. The fact that it is tinged with gray indicates that as a very young child she was often frightened. There was nothing in her home life or in her experience to cause her fears; they were not of anything specific, but rather a kind of intangible haunting dread of the dark unknown that many children seem to suffer from. Instinctual and semi-conscious, such fears are often the carry-over from a forgotten past. The dark blue anchor-like symbol below her feet shows that these intangible fears became tangible in her dream-life. When I asked if she had had recurrent nightmares, she remembered them clearly even though she no longer suffered from them. Over the years, her fears had crystallized into this symbol, but the fact that its position lies so low shows that they had almost entirely left her, and remained only as a shadow in her unconscious mind.

At the edges of her aura you will see the blue bands that always indicate strain, similar to those in #9 and #12. As in those cases, the strain seems to have been long-standing and probably originated in her early fears. She was apt to force herself beyond her limits of nervous and physical endurance, because she had no notion what these limits were. The stress had now become quite deep-seated, to the point where her nervous tension was causing her to have periodic bouts of severe headache, accompanied by nausea. Otherwise her health was very good.

A bit higher, on the left, the color becomes slightly bluer. This indicates that she was willful as a child and probably succeeded in getting her own way, for her parents were kind and affectionate and often spoiled her, although she was unaware of the fact. She was an only child who spent much of her time with adults, and she was therefore quite precocious. Indeed, save for the fact that she was sometimes lonely for the companionship of other children, her early surroundings were ideal.

Farther above, the green lightens and becomes tinged with yellow. This shows that even when quite young she thought about the things around her, and used her mind in her daily life as well as in her studies. As the color becomes more yellow, it indicates a conscious effort to control her selfishness, as well as to understand whatever she was working on. The patch of orange is an incipient form of the plumes you have already seen in #7, #11 and #13. As I said before, this color always indicates strong convictions and a degree of intellectual pride in having arrived at what one considers to be the truth. From early adolescence this girl had been searching for some teaching that would satisfy her unanswered questions, and when she was introduced to Buddhism, theosophy and Eastern philosophy she was convinced she had found those answers. This orange patch had not yet solidified into a plume; whether it would become more rigid as life went on, or gradually relax and disappear, was as yet problematical.

This young woman had recently given birth to a baby, and the event quite naturally occupied a great deal of her attention. You will see this child's face in her green band, because she not only spent time caring for him physically but also thought a good deal about his progress. She was determined to be a good mother—a determination which made her somewhat overanxious. The green band itself is of a clear color, which denotes sympathy, and is fairly wide, showing that she was deft with her hands. She had no special artistic talent, but she did not find it difficult to teach herself to do various things, such as sewing, gardening, playing a musical instrument or using tools of various kinds. Also within the green band you will see various yellow geometrical forms, all of which relate to her intellectual interests, while the blue rounds and spirals again reflect the use of her will to control her thoughts and feelings.

Pink is a color prominent in her aura, both above and below, showing that she had a great deal of affection, not only for her family but also for all sorts of other people. The pink above the green band, which is purer in color, is a kind of generalized feeling which reflects the ideals she had with regard to her emotional life, while the patch below shows the affection she expressed day by day. The small cones and spirals in this color again reveal her anxiety that she might not succeed in living up to her ideals, but these were temporary and would pass away.

Yellow appears in two places in her upper aura, and shows her innate intelligence and her capacity for real thought, even with respect to difficult and intricate subjects. The yellow just above the pink represents the power of mind she drew on regularly, while the streak of yellow higher up on the left is the more abstract or theoretical aspect that was not so much in use. The area of blue-green on the right side is related, as always, to aesthetics; in her case it does not represent artistic ability so much as sensibility—an appreciation of beauty and harmony as universal ideals. As always, the lavender at the top of the aura indicates a person's innate spirituality. In her case, it is connected to the golden yellow on the left and to the blue-green on the right, showing that both her search for meaning and her appreciation of beauty were related to her spiritual quest. The darker violet is a composite emotion—an intuitional approach to understanding the inner order, meaning and purpose behind the phenomena of nature.

14A. Fifty-six years later

These aura pictures were made so long ago that almost all of the adults are now dead. This woman, however, is still very much alive, and it might be interesting to trace her development. When the picture was made she was still on the threshold of life, and her potentials were just beginning to unfold. Now that she is a woman over eighty, she is still vigorous and alert, and has lost little of her energy. Although

14a. Fifty-Six Years Later

retired, she remains active; in addition to her intellectual interests she is on the Boards of a number of charitable organizations. She has been happily married for almost sixty years, and has a large family of children and grandchildren with whom she is on excellent terms.

Her sense of purpose has not diminished, and she has always continued her practice of meditation. Blessed with good health and good karma (for her life has been singularly free of problems and difficulties), she has been able to pursue her goals without any friction in her family relationships. She no longer feels the need to exercise her will so strongly upon herself, and because of this, she is much more relaxed. The anxiety caused by her childhood fears has vanished, and she has outgrown most of her strain and tension. Consequently, her nervous headaches have long since disappeared, and her health is excellent.

The colors of her aura have become softer, lighter and more balanced. (The aura in #14A was recently painted by another artist, not Juanita Donahoo.) The orange patch has diminished in size, since she no longer feels the need to defend her ideas so vigorously. The pink below is balanced by a paler pink above, showing that her affection is still strong, but more detached. The yellow in the upper aura is wider and now lies adjacent to the green band, indicating that her intellectual abilities and interests have deepened and become more active. The lavender above the head has widened a great deal through study and meditation, showing that her spiritual insight has increased. As a result of her years of meditation, the wings of dark blue which were so prominent a feature of her aura have spread out to form a half-circle of purple which links her higher energies with her mind and emotions.

All in all, the colors of her aura have become much more diffuse, and as a result her aura is more harmonious.

Thinking about this woman's aura, and comparing it with that of the other old lady, #8, has led me to consider the aging process as it affects one's emotional health and vigor. If you refer back to #8, you will remember that the lower part of that old lady's aura was filmed with gray, due to her diminished energies and the fact that she lived so much in the past. Yet she had been a very vital and active person all her life. Her flagging energies may have been due to a loss of physical vitality, but also in part, I believe, to the loss of her mental and emotional stimulus. Hers was the same problem that faces many people who are forced to retire: her work was taken away from her. Whether this occurs because of age, ill health or other circumstances, it is an event which sometimes can have traumatic consequences. Some people lose their sense of purpose, and with it the confidence that they can still make a contribution—and this confidence is vital to one's self-esteem. I shall be talking about this question in detail in Chapter IX, but the comment has bearing on the aging process.

In contrast, #14 is still leading a full and active life, with many intellectual interests. Thus her mental and emotional energies supplement whatever diminution might naturally occur in her physical strength and vitality due to her age. Doctors routinely urge their elderly patients to keep active, both physically and mentally, and my observations fully support this advice. In Chapter II I stressed the fact that the higher energies can modify and transform the lower. Because the mind and emotions work closely with the etheric, mental energy can and does vitalize the physical body.

In our culture, unfortunately, old age is usually dreaded. In contrast, in the East it is regarded as a period when the lessening of responsibilities gives leisure for contemplation and for the enjoyment of nature. Free of the necessity always to be doing, one can let go and be oneself. When old age is accepted as a stage of life which brings its own benefits, the gifts of equanimity, of quietness and of detachment can enrich the end of an active life.

VII
The Effects of Illness

The effects of illness are readily visible in the aura, especially when the condition is chronic or has been of long duration. Every disease has its own pattern, but there is always a diminution of energy, which results in a general graying or muting of the brilliancy of the colors, and a tendency of the whole aura to droop. There are frequently signs of stress, which come from the effort to carry on in spite of pain and weakness.

In a healthy person, there is a natural outflow of emotional energy, which not only permits a free interaction with others but also prevents the internal blockages which can lead to emotional inhibition and depression. Illness, however, tends to turn one inward, since it always makes claims on a person's attention. It takes conscious effort to endure pain, and a lack of energy drains the ability to function normally. The result is a condition of strain.

In diagnosing and treating illness, I work primarily at the etheric level, which as I have said is both the counterpart of the physical body and the precursor of illness. But emotional factors are very important in healing. This will be discussed in more detail in Chapter IX, but the pictures that follow here show clearly the degree to which illness is an emotional as well as a physical condition. Since this is so, a negative attitude can aggravate sickness; I would not say that a positive attitude can cure, but it certainly helps the patient to cooperate in the healing process, and thus makes treatment more effective.

15. *The Results of Polio*

Our first picture is of one of Dr. Bengtsson's clinic patients, and since it was her habit never to tell me anything about their condition beforehand, I knew nothing of this girl's history. When I came into the room, she was already sitting down and her disability was not obvious. Yet one glance was enough to show me how sick and weak she was, and what effort it took for her just to keep going.

This poor girl had had an attack of polio when she was two years old, which left her physically crippled and neurologically damaged. She was now twenty-two and quite plump and heavy, so that walking was very difficult for her. She might have been able to adjust to the effects of the polio, but her condition was further complicated by severe chronic asthma, which was a serious illness.

Looking at her picture, you will see that the edges of her aura are wavy and uneven, and that they have lost their definition except at the extreme top and bottom. The whole aura is draped in a tenuous cloud of gray which covers the energy valves, and these themselves are open, shallow, flaccid, and much paler than they should be. Their rhythmic pulsations were also irregular, although of course this cannot be shown in the picture. All of these aberrations indicated that the mechanism which controlled her intake and rejection of emotional energy was not functioning normally. Because the valves were so open she was inadequately protected from outside pressures, and was not able to throw off emotions easily. Thus she had little resistance, and tired so easily that she was in a state of chronic exhaustion.

When I first looked at her, I was struck by the gray cloud shot with red which covers the whole upper part of her body, including the solar plexus region. (You will see something similar in cases #9 and #16.) I realized that this was a temporary condition and of recent origin, so I asked her whether she had had an injection lately. She replied that she had been feeling weak and nervous on the way to our appointment, and had therefore given herself a shot of adrenaline. This was very interesting to me, because the color gray in the aura indicates fear and depression, while red is caused by anger, and adrenaline is secreted by the body under the stress of fear and anger. Thus the effect of the injection on her aura was to simulate these emotions.

The qualities which always show themselves in the upper part of the aura are in her case very nebulous. Since she had had practically no opportunity to develop her potentials, they were weak and ineffectual. On the other hand, by far the most dominant color in her aura is the strong blue of will, which is the expression of her higher self. This blue pours from the top of her aura right down the spine through her chakras and into her green band. The shade of this color in the picture is not quite accurate, for it should be lighter and more luminous than the blue colors which appear lower down. The higher blue represents her tremendous determination to live as normally as possible—the will to overcome her handicaps and accomplish something in the physical world.

You will see that her green band is both pale and narrow, a natural result of her inability to do any kind of work. But the blue of her will is reflected in the broad band of darker blue just below the green band, which shows the force of the struggle she continually waged to keep going. When you are so weak and low in energy, even the effort to put one foot in front of the other requires real stamina. It took strength of will for her to move, to walk, to lift things and even to breathe, and in addition she had to endure almost constant pain. This wide strip of blue shows the strength of her effort.

The three blue bands which curve around low down in the aura on the left side also reflect this effort, but they show the results of stress even more plainly. Her struggle to resist the effects of almost continuous pain and to follow the doctors' orders had resulted in a more or less permanent condition of strain. She was trying hard to use her will power to compensate at least in part for her physical disabilities, but since she so often failed in what she was trying to do, these bands alternate with the dark gray of depression.

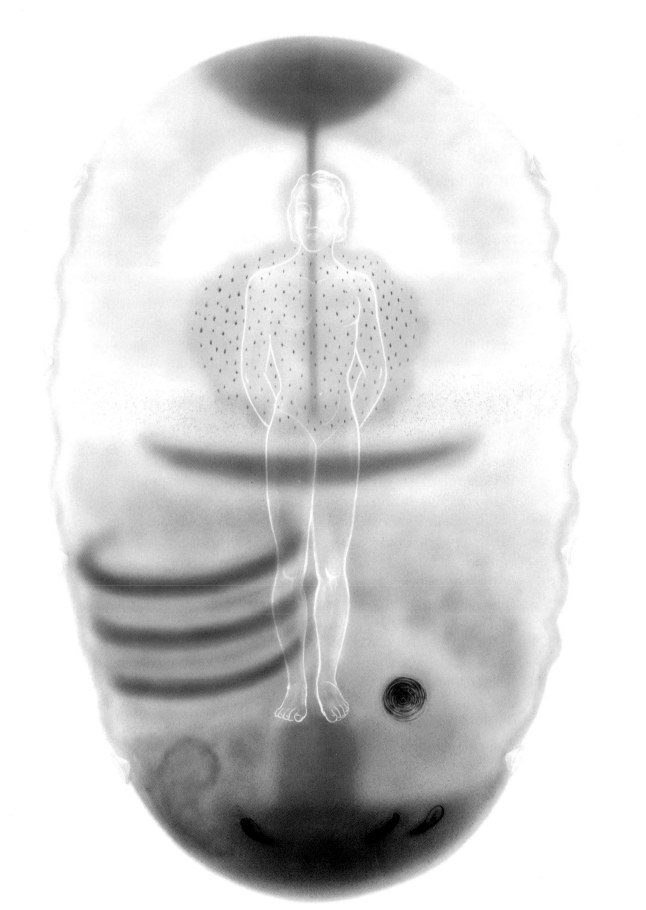

15. The Results of Polio

There is a large area of pink across the upper part of her aura, and this is reflected in a darker shade below, indicating that she was a really affectionate girl. But here again the color is blocked at the edges of her aura, because she had no outlet for her emotions. Outside the members of her immediate family — who were good and kind to her — she had little contact with anyone besides her doctors. Since her energy was so low she could only interact with people for short periods, and she had difficulty in expressing her feelings at any time. She would try tentatively to reach out and do things with others, but she soon became exhausted and had to give up.

Because of her inability to go to school, she had had only the rudiments of an education and little incentive to develop her mind. The fact that the yellow above her head does not extend to the edges of the aura shows that she had very little ability to focus her mind upon a subject. Her attention span was poor, and she became restless when she tried to concentrate for any length of time. Because of her family's limited resources, she had a very narrow environment and little mental stimulus. She had vague yearnings but did not know how to focus them, and since she was completely untrained, she had very little confidence that she could ever really accomplish anything.

There is a great deal of gray in the lower part of her aura, mixed with green: green, because her past was full of things she had tried to do, and gray because her attempts usually ended in failure. The marks in the gray beneath her feet are related to memories of these past frustrations; they represent discouragement and depression. The patch of blue-green on the lower right side of her aura near the feet is the result of an early period in her life when she was somewhat better physically and was inspired to try to do more. The rosy red symbol within that color is a latent memory of a person who encouraged her at that time, and who made a great impression on her. The blue-green plume on the lower left echoes this early effort, which unfortunately again resulted in failure. The whole sad record of her life is one of trying and failing again and again, so that it was remarkable she still had the will to go on.

The mixture of colors in the lower part of her aura indicates that she had had a desire to be somebody (the orange patch), but was also frequently overcome by feelings of inferiority (the gray-green). Somewhat higher on the right, the green shot with gray and pink shows her efforts to make herself do as many things as possible, but the colors are vague and indeterminate because her capacity was so low.

This was a very sick girl, whose ability to function at all was seriously handicapped by her chronic asthma. Because of this, she was continually in and out of hospital, but when she did go in her low level of resistance made her vulnerable to infection, and she was apt to pick up some other illness. Thus her condition was complicated by all sorts of secondary ailments.

But she had a great deal of determination. I do not believe that she was born with so much will power; she had developed it as a result of her tremendous efforts to overcome her handicaps — even if these efforts met with only slight success. Drawing upon the strength of her spiritual will — which is always responsive to one's efforts — she had persisted in her determination to get better and to use her faculties as much as she possibly could. This was a real achievement.

Trying to help and encourage her, I suggested that her stamina and resistance to disease might be improved if she would study more. The effort to use her mind would draw upon her higher energies, and it could improve her self-esteem and reduce her depression. I also thought it would be helpful if she were to visualize some of the things she might be able to do, rather than dwell upon those she could not. In this way, she might be able to draw upon the higher level energies of the mind to enhance her physical strength.

I also suggested that if she were to leave New York for a drier climate her breathing might improve, and this in turn would make it easier for her to focus her thoughts. She followed my advice and moved to Arizona, where I believe her asthma was somewhat better, but I subsequently lost touch with her. Thus I do not know whether she was able to follow my suggestions for developing the potentialities of her mind.

16. A Child Born with Down's Syndrome

This is the aura of a little boy about seven years of age who suffered from Down's syndrome, a genetic defect caused by an abnormality of the chromosomes. It is characterized by mental deficiency and a generally oriental appearance; for this reason it has been called mongolism. Strictly speaking, this child is handicapped, not diseased, but he belongs in this group because the abnormalities in his aura parallel his physical abnormalities quite closely.

First of all you will see that the shape of the aura is much rounder than that of #4, who is a normal boy of seven; it is more like that of the three-year-old girl. This shows that he was not maturing at the normal rate. All the middle and lower part of his aura is draped in a grayish cloud somewhat similar to that in the previous picture, although the effect is not quite so severe. But the energy intake valves are affected; their action is sluggish and dull, and thus both the child's level of energy and his resistance are impaired. There is an unusual amount of gray in the aura, but in this case it comes from weakness, poor health and lack of energy, rather than from fear or depression.

If you compare this boy's aura with those of the other children, you will see that the unfolding bands of color which represent his potentialities all droop downward quite sharply and are edged with gray. This is another sign of his general inability to function normally, or to express himself. At the top of the aura the colors which should reveal his higher faculties are so vague as to be almost imperceptible, and the gray which overshadows the yellow indicates that at birth there was an almost complete blankness of mind.

Interestingly enough, the absence of the usual brown of selfishness at the bottom of the aura reflects this blankness. As I have said, all normal children are busy asserting themselves, since they begin quite early to develop an ego. But this poor boy was lacking the mental capacity to have a sense of self, and thus be selfish. In him, the bottom of the aura is filled with the dark blue-gray of stress, whose effects extend upward into the active part of the aura.

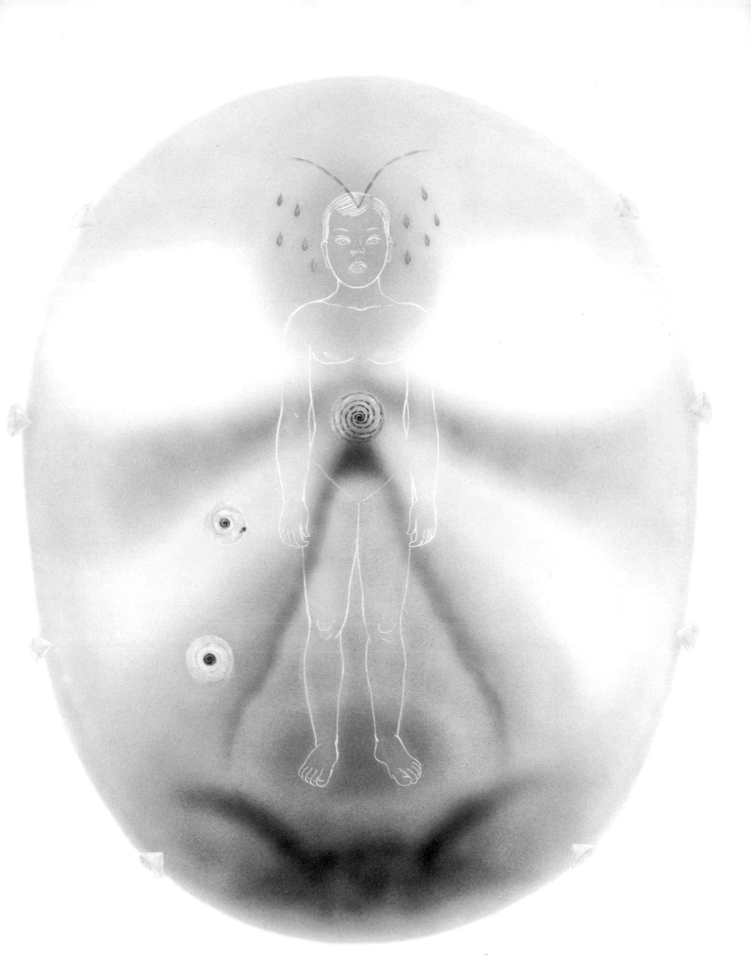

16. A Child Born with Down's Syndrome

The large areas of yellow in the upper aura might mislead you into attributing it to the presence of mental ability, but the color is extremely vague and its position is much too low, almost below his head. He was quite seriously deficient mentally, but he was not entirely without intelligence, and he showed some signs of trying to reach out and communicate with those around him. The cloud surrounding his head is the result of some injections he was being given daily in an effort to improve his thinking processes, and the sparks of yellow within the cloud indicate that the medication was producing some mental stimulus, although this might have been of short duration. The injections were part of an experimental program that was being tried out at that time, and I am not sure how successful it was.

The pink in this little boy's aura is the most normal of his colors. As is typical of Down's syndrome children, he had an affectionate nature and was quite responsive to those who were caring for him. His green band is very pale and slants down sharply, showing that his physical coordination was poor. He found it difficult to do the simplest physical tasks, such as dressing himself, because there was no coordination between mind and hand.

In the middle of the green band, centered over the solar plexus chakra, there is a circular blue disk. This is one of his karmic indicators. It is in an active or unfolded state, rather than latent like the others we have seen, because his physical handicap, which was the result of karma, began at birth and was dominating his life. Its position at the top of the green band shows, on the one hand, that his karma was related to his inability to function in the world; on the other, that the solar plexus chakra, which is central to the distribution of emotional energy, was very disorganized. This suggested to me that his glandular system was out of order. The other two karmic indicators were also related to his disabilities, but they were not as yet active.

The bands of blue that seem to issue from his solar plexus center and sweep downwards to his feet indicate that his strain and lack of energy were related to this center. They seem to enclose a separate area of pale green, but this is actually a continuation of his green band, which was fractured by these lines of strain. The pale cloud of orange-brown around his feet lies within these blue lines, indicating that his incipient sense of self-confidence was constrained by his physical handicap.

Though badly impaired, this little boy did have the good fortune of having been placed in the care of a foster parent who was sincerely fond of him. This relationship had not only stimulated his natural affection, but also had over the years fostered in him a certain degree of mental integration.

My recommendations were that the boy should be encouraged to do simple physical tasks that he might enjoy, such as taking care of plants. This might help to develop his mental and physical coordination. While he would never be normal, he might be trained to do some simple work, like gardening, which would not require much thought.

As I never received any further reports about this child, I do not know whether he improved, or whether he died young, as is so often the case with those suffering from Down's syndrome. His karma seemed to be related to a life of frustration from the point of view of inner development.

17. An Acute Anxiety State

This is the picture of a man in his fifties who was in the midst of what is commonly called a nervous breakdown. It would not have taken a clairvoyant to perceive this, for when he came to see me he was in a state of intense nervous agitation. He was a forceful personality, and had achieved a good deal in his life, as the strong colors in his aura indicate. But at the time this picture was painted he was not able to accomplish anything, for he was trapped in his own anxiety to the point where he even doubted his ability to think.

This man had been interested in Eastern thought for many years and had accepted its fundamental precepts, but at this moment he was full of doubt and uncertainty, and these ideas retained very little meaning for him. He was fundamentally a good man who had lost his way, and with it, his sense of self-identity. He had had a very successful business which was going steadily downhill, and this situation naturally aggravated his anxiety and accelerated the breakdown of his self-confidence.

All this fear and stress can be seen quite plainly in his aura, most dramatically in the two blue shells which enclose him. The nervous strain he was suffering from caused the outer band at the edges of his aura, which is similar to those we have seen elsewhere but rises much higher in the aura than any of the others. The second, inner shell is even more serious, for it had created a barrier which inhibited the normal outward flow of his emotions and turned their energies inward upon himself. When people suffer from such a condition they cannot express their emotions; they may start to feel something, but then their uncertainty will make them hesitate and pull back.

In his case, the blockage was increasing his stress day by day. Like a spinning skater or a squirrel in a cage, his anxiety kept gaining momentum because of this tight, repetitive, circular action. The fact that the blockage extends so high in his aura shows that his higher faculties were also constrained. Sadly, he was shut off in two directions—from the outer world and from his inner self. This affected his mental balance, and the resulting loss of perspective led him into false interpretations of the events in his daily life. This further increased his emotional and mental agitation. He was, in fact, caught in a trap built of his own pressures, his loss of contact with reality, and his distorted imagination.

The areas of pink in his aura indicate that this man was by nature affectionate, but the pale shade of the color shows his inability to share his feelings. You can see how enclosed the pink is, both above and below the green band. He still loved his wife and children, but he told me with tears in his eyes that he absolutely could not express his feeling, or go out to them in any way. He had been preoccupied with his business for such a long time, and working so hard, that he had grown away from his family. Yet the fundamental cause of his over-

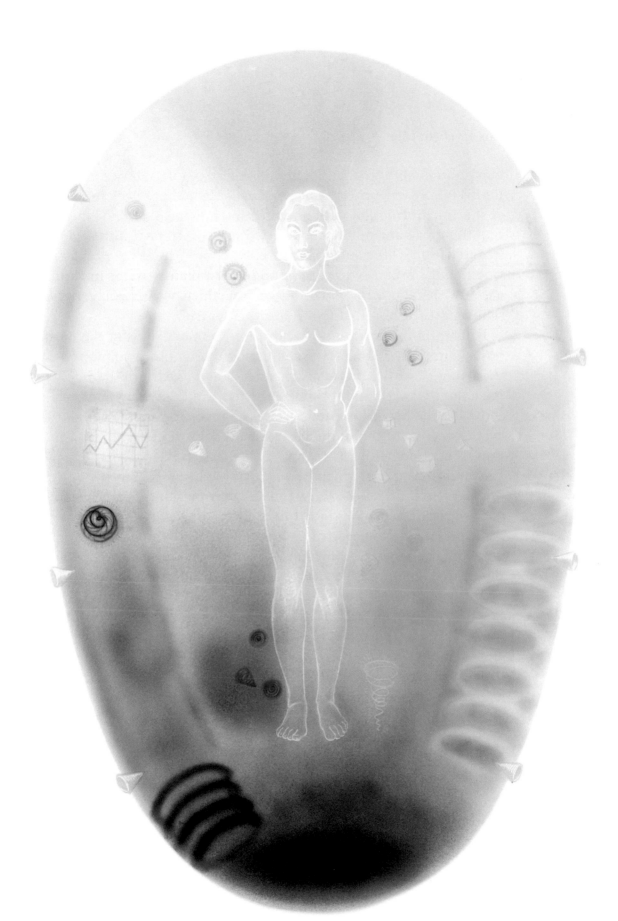

17. An Acute Anxiety State

work and the pressure he put on himself arose out of his desire to care for his family and provide for them well. He had not been in the habit of sharing his troubles with his wife, and now he could no longer feel that there was any relationship between them. In fact, his family only irritated him. This troubled him deeply, because he felt guilty; he worried about his family's future, and felt frustrated by his inability to care for them. All the pink and yellow whirls which you can see in many parts of his aura relate to these worries.

Frustration was not new to him, for there are signs at the bottom of his aura that he had had such periods when quite young. He had not had an easy life financially, and had had to earn his living by doing a number of different things. The red bands low down in the aura show that he had often been angry and annoyed, and although these experiences belonged to the past, he had not forgotten all the opposition he had met with. In a sense, these marks reflect the earlier struggles and difficulties which had constrained him in the past, just as the lines of blue reflect the strain he was presently experiencing.

His green band is of a good width, and its yellow hue shows that his work had always been of an intellectual kind, but again, it is filled with the yellow vortices which indicate worry. All the yellow above shows that in the past he had been both intelligent and innovative, able to concentrate and think things through carefully. Within the green band there is a large graph-like form, a symbol of order. It is the enduring impression of his life's work, and epitomizes his greatest achievement. He had been one of the first people in the United States to create the standards and develop the method of taking public opinion polls — an enterprise which was later taken over by Gallup and other organizations. He did in fact write several books on the subject. As the symbol in his green band implies, his tendency was to categorize everything, for not only was this the way he earned his living, it was the way his mind functioned normally. He was happiest when he could reduce everything around him into an orderly pattern. The same might have been said about #13, yet there was a vast difference between the two men, for this one's type of order was mechanical and statistical, whereas the other's was archetypal and universal.

At the time that I saw this man, he had recently had to give up his business, and the cessation of its pressures left him completely bereft. He had lost the sense of direction which his work had afforded him, and he was beset by worry and uncertainty. His anxiety had been developing for several years, and by the time I saw him he was in such a bad state that he was overwhelmed by his dilemmas and unable to make any decisions. Sadly, he was really beyond help, and in fact he died within a short time. It was a tragic case.

I wish I could say that this man's case was rare, but unfortunately this is not so. In fact, it is more typical of today's world than of the time when the painting was made. There are many men and women who are fundamentally caring and well-motivated, but in whom the pressures of their careers and their desire for success have forced their families into the background. This always makes for strained and difficult relations.

In all too many people, the habit of living and working under extreme pressure creates patterns of stress which eventually end in burnout, and this can have a very damaging effect upon their families and all their personal relationships. This is why it is so important to learn to watch for signs of stress within oneself, and take steps to change negative emotional patterns before they take their toll.

18. The Effects of Meditation upon a Chronic Heart Patient

This is the aura of a remarkable Russian lady in her forties, who had been born with a heart so enlarged that the doctors who examined her from time to time were surprised to find her still alive. Yet she had survived a period of great danger and anguish, and although always an invalid, she was happily married and lived another thirty years after this picture was made. She was, in fact, a medical miracle.

At first glance, one might not believe that this was the aura of a sick person, because although muted, the colors are remarkably clear. The whole aura displays a general symmetry and balance, for the colors of the upper part are to a large extent reflected below, a sign of personal integration. The gray of fear and depression so common in the chronically ill is visible in the lower aura, but the upper part remains unclouded. Yet this is the aura of a woman who had for years lived with a severe heart condition that caused her continual pain.

You will see that the green band droops down sharply at the edges, a clear sign that her energies are not flowing normally. Moreover, the blue of strain not only clouds the lower part of her aura but extends upward through the green band itself, thus directly affecting all her activities. I have said before that this condition is present when a person is being forced beyond the ordinary limits of nervous or physical endurance. This woman was not of a nervous temperament, however, and her stress was entirely related to a lack of energy resulting from her illness. All her emotional expression was tinged with strain. Since she had no reserves of strength to meet any sudden calls upon her, she had to husband her energies very carefully. Everything she did required an effort of will.

The fact that this aura is free from many of the signs of illness is due in large part to the fact that for years she had been regularly practicing meditation. Every day she made a conscious effort to free herself from the emotional restrictions which illness so often imposes, and to reach out to others in love and affection. The most prominent color in her aura is pink, showing that she not only had a great deal of affection in her nature but also that she projected it intentionally in her meditation, and sought to carry it through into expression in her personal relationships.

The clear blue and violet at the top of her aura indicate her devotion to spiritual ideals, and their expanse shows that she tried to practice these ideals in her daily life. The large area of green which balances the pink in the upper part of her aura testifies to her sympathetic attitude towards others, as well as her response to what she perceived as the innate beauty and harmony of the world.

The position of the yellow in the upper aura, as well as its shade, shows that she liked to think and was by no means unintelligent, but it also indicates that the action of her mind was engaged with ab-

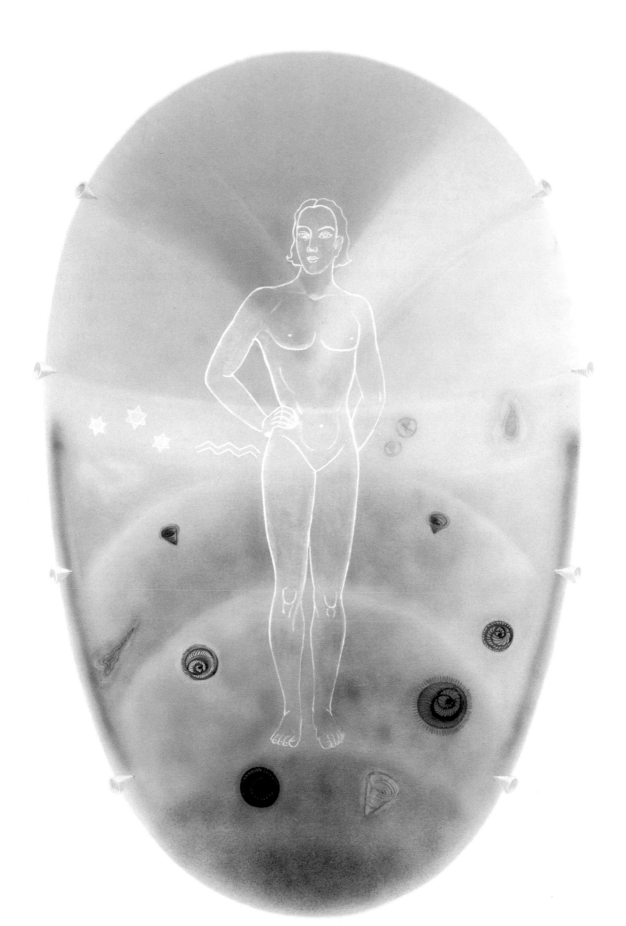

18. *The Effects of Meditation upon
a Chronic Heart Patient*

stract ideas rather than with the solution of practical problems. This was her natural inclination and it was fortified by her illness, for she led a sheltered life in which all her ordinary needs were well cared for and did not need to be thought about.

As I have said, her green band shows her lack of physical strength, and her inability to do any active work. The pink flame in the band results from her efforts to bring her affection through into her daily life, and her unconscious perception that her real work in the world was concerned with people, and with her ability to help them through kindness and sympathy. The yellow stars are related to her interest in symbolic thought, which engaged her mind regularly.

The lower part of her aura testifies to the fact that her inner tranquillity had been won through conscious effort, and was certainly not the result of the physical circumstances she was born into. The blue-gray at the bottom of her aura, just above the usual brown of selfishness, shows that her childhood must have been filled with uncertainty and fear. There are two large, painful scars within this blue-gray background, indicating that when she was around twenty-five or thirty she must have gone through a period of great distress, during which she had to bear some tremendous burden. These scars have a kind of double action. They show that on the one hand she was trying to keep steady, since she felt that everything depended on her, and at the same time she was desperate because she didn't know what she ought to do.

The gray which overlays the green shows that although she did take action, it was colored by fear and strain. These experiences were so traumatic that they might well have continued to influence her the rest of her life. The interesting thing is that although they still lingered in her unconscious mind, the practice of meditation had enabled her to push them down into the past, so that they were no longer active in her.

The patch of orange with a whirl in it shows that the events of her life had to some degree given her a sense of inadequacy and inferiority. This occasionally caused her to react somewhat aggressively, especially in defense of those she was most fond of. A response of this kind was really not compatible with her temperament, however, and the continued effects of her meditation probably dissipated it in time. She was a person who understood life more through a kind of sympathetic perception than by means of conscious thought, so that in a way she did not so much solve problems as dissolve them.

To a remarkable degree, this woman's aura is a record both of her past trauma and of her present state of peace and harmony. Having grown up in Czarist Russia, she went through the terrors of the Revolution, when as a young student she suffered the loss of friends and family. She barely managed to escape to Turkey, where she was imprisoned and underwent many hardships. She finally succeeded in reaching the United States, but her troubles were not over, for she was without resources and had to earn her own living in addition to adjusting to a very different way of life.

All these difficulties were complicated by her illness, and yet she managed not only to survive but to remain in control of her circumstances. Part of her secret was her natural serenity. She was not overwhelmed by the problems of her life because she always felt the strength of a spiritual presence that could carry her through her difficulties. Her sense of this presence grew and deepened through her meditation.

She had the great good fortune, later in life, to marry a kind and capable man whom she adored. They were everything to one another. Not only did he share all her interests, but he was very practical and self-reliant, and delighted in relieving her of the burdens of living. So although she was in constant pain, she otherwise lived in ideal circumstances. Although she had to be alone a good deal during the day, she was never lonely, because she had many friends in the Russian community who visited her when she was confined to bed. They told her all their troubles and actively sought her advice, so that her affectionate sympathy found a constant outlet and avenue of expression. Thus she lived a remarkably full life in spite of being an invalid.

She was thoroughly aware of her physical limitations, and learned to husband her resources and manage her expenditures of energy remarkably well. When she felt ill, she went to bed, sometimes for weeks on end. Through her meditation she learned how to relax and remain calm when she was in pain. In the same way, she opened herself to higher energies which helped her to regulate her body, and these sustained her to the end of her life.

She herself was convinced that her meditation had kept her alive and functioning far beyond expectations. I have always felt that her life was an example of the ways in which it is possible to work with one's karma and achieve one's goal in life in spite of what might appear to be insuperable difficulties.

III
Possibilities for Change and Growth

VIII
Healing and the Practice
of Visualization

For most of my life I have been interested in the phenomenon of healing, and it is now the main focus of my work. Over the years, I have
fortunately been able to watch a number of well-known practitioners
at work, and thus observe different aspects of the healing process as
it is taking place. As a result of this experience, about eighteen years
ago Dr. Dolores Krieger, Professor of Nursing at New York University, and I developed a technique called Therapeutic Touch. This
method is now used by thousands of nurses and health professionals
in hospitals both in the United States and abroad, and it has been written about extensively.[1]

Techniques of healing are not the subject of this book. But since
the word "healing" means to make whole, it applies to problems of
emotional dysfunction as well as to physical disease. These all affect
the aura in different ways. When we speak of healing in the general
sense as the restoration of wholeness, we have to include the possibility of self-healing in addition to intervention by non-medical as well
as medical procedures.

---

1. Dr. Krieger's account of the development of this healing method was first published in her groundbreaking book, *Therapeutic Touch*, and has been followed by
many other accounts. A simple, straightforward description of the procedures can
be found in *Therapeutic Touch, A Practical Guide*, by Janet Macrae (Alfred A.
Knopf, New York, 1988). Another book which might be of interest is *Spiritual Aspects
of the Healing Arts*, of which I am the Editor (Theosophical Publishing House,
Wheaton, Ill., 1985).

As I have tried to show, mind and emotions play a constant, determining role in health and disease. It therefore seems appropriate to focus briefly upon the interaction which takes place when one human being is trying to help another who is sick or otherwise in trouble. When a person is sick, the interplay between the physical body and the etheric energetic system is affected. At the same time there is a reflection of the physical pain in the emotions, because the memory of pain and the fear of its recurrence come at this level. Those who have been practicing healing methods such as Therapeutic Touch for a long time may get an impression of where the patient feels the pain, and this also indicates whatever disturbance there may be at the emotional level. Therefore, to understand something about the healing process it is necessary to appreciate the relationship between the emotions and the etheric energy field.

Etheric Energy

In Chapter II I briefly mentioned that the etheric is the energetic prototype of the physical body. This being so, there are etheric counterparts of the various organs. The etheric energy flows normally through these organs in a stable pattern, and any disruption in this flow pattern is an indication of disease. If a person is in good health, the flow among all the organs (and between the etheric chakras) is rhythmic, but when the disease process has taken hold there is a break in the pattern in the area where the problem lies.

From my experience, another indication of illness is a general diminution or narrowing of the stream of energy; an analogy would be a stream where debris has partially dammed the riverbed and prevented the water from flowing normally. Thus one can often perceive where the disease is occurring by noting the reduction in the flow of energy through the various organs of the body. But because of the constant emotional/etheric interaction, emotional response also has a similar effect.

To take an example, anxiety can be an overpowering emotion which for the time being obscures all our other feelings. Even when we realize that the anxiety is out of proportion to its cause, we are often unable to rid ourselves of the irrational fear. Anxiety is always an inhibiting factor, for the concentration of feelings and thoughts upon just one subject creates an emotional vortex, and this in turn reduces the free flow of energy within the aura. (Such vortices can be seen in several of the aura pictures.) An emotional pattern of this kind has a draining effect upon the energies of the whole body. In addition, the stress caused by anxiety affects the solar plexus chakra directly, and acts through it upon the adrenals and the pancreas. Thus an important aspect of healing is the reduction of the inhibiting effects of a patient's fear.

The Healing Attitude

In all the interactions of healing, the development of empathy, or sensitivity, is most important, for the primary contact with the person we are trying to help is at the emotional level. Therefore the first requirement for a healer is a genuine feeling of compassion and a desire to help the person who is sick or in pain, for without this it would be very difficult to engender a feeling of empathy with the patient. What I have said elsewhere about interpersonal relationships applies here with special force, for in the practice of healing the rapport between healer and patient is a significant factor.

As it is practiced today among nurses and other health professionals, healing is an art which is not undertaken casually. It requires a moment or two of self-preparation which is based upon what we call centering, that is, a conscious effort to free oneself from one's anxieties and inner disturbances, and to be at peace within oneself.

I always teach this practice of centering as a preparation for healing as well as in meditation, in which connection I shall speak of it again. If we are upset and in a state of inner turmoil, we may try to reach out and send feelings of compassion to the patient, but the effort may be distorted by an undercurrent of turbulent emotion.

Through centering, we become aware of our own disturbed emotions and consciously disassociate ourselves from them by focusing all our energies in the heart center, which is the seat of compassion and of wholeness. This fosters two qualities which are important in the healing process: rootedness and detachment.

Centering not only makes us feel at peace; it also connects us with the inner order within ourselves. This I call rootedness. By concentrating on being peaceful within, we align ourselves with the fundamental order and compassion which are expressions of the spiritual component of the world. Healing is the reestablishment of order within the body's systems. I perceive its accomplishment as due to a universal energy which springs from the tendency towards order that is at the heart of all living processes. Therefore, if it is possible for individuals who are ill to achieve the emotional balance produced by positive feelings, so that the flow of emotional energy is not constricted, as in #17, but flows outward, as in #18, this will not in itself effect a cure, but it will help to produce a state conducive to healing.

When we are trying to help someone (and this interaction can take place within the family as well as between a health professional and a patient), it is always important to realize that the results are not in our hands. Healing involves forces and agencies which we do not fully understand, and certainly cannot command. Rather, we seek to be instruments of the power of healing which exists everywhere in nature. Even in the orthodox sense, medical procedures do not cure the patient; they merely remove the impediments to healing, which the body itself must accomplish. Therefore, the healer must scrupulously avoid any trace of vested interest in the outcome of his or her efforts in behalf of another. The end cannot be predicted, and success is not the goal. Whatever the results of our efforts may be, we must accept them without blame or credit. This realization promotes detachment, that is, freedom from attachment to the results of our own actions.

Since the healing energy is a beneficent power available to all living beings, the ability to draw upon it does not depend upon religious belief. Every person who practices healing may conceptualize it differently. Most of the well-known healers have credited their powers to God, and tied them to a specific faith. This is important for the individual, since it makes the practice of healing part of one's belief system and cultural background. I personally feel that since this healing power or energy is available to everyone, it is essentially the same, no matter how it may be described. Therefore there should be a basic unity and cooperation between practitioners of all the healing techniques — a situation that becomes more possible as the validity of the art is more widely recognized among health professionals.

Qualifications for the Healer

I have been asked whether special qualifications are needed in order to become a healer, or whether anyone can learn. In reply I always emphasize that healing is a learning process. Certainly a large number of nurses who seemed to be without any special qualifications have learned to practice Therapeutic Touch very skillfully. Although the great healers may have been endowed with an unusual degree of sensitivity, the ability to heal can be acquired to some degree by anyone who tries sincerely and faithfully to develop the faculty. Thus to the requirements of compassion and sensitivity, which I have already mentioned, I should add another: consistent effort.

No matter what technique is used, a healer usually tries to send energy wherever there is a destructive pattern. This helps to strengthen that particular part of the patient's body to heal itself. But even while working on a disturbed area at the physical/etheric level, the healer should be constantly aware of the emotions as well, for the patient must be thought of as entirely whole. It should always be remembered that although the healing is intended to re-establish a harmonious relationship between body, mind and emotions, this accomplishment stems from our access to a level deeper than either the mind or the emotions — the spiritual dimension from which the healing energy springs.

The Role of the Chakras

While the effects of disease show up plainly in the aura, as the pictures have shown, the chakras are also affected, and therefore they too play an important role in healing. As I mentioned in Chapter IV, stressful emotions can affect the whole digestive system — including the spleen, the liver and the pancreas--through the solar plexus chakra. When healing energy is sent to this chakra the whole region is energized, and at the same time the patient's anxiety and fear are reduced. Therefore work on this area is usually a routine practice in healing.

Interaction at the emotional level may be initiated through the solar plexus, but of course it comes through the aura and the etheric field as well for it is impossible to separate the two functions. Actually, the energy pours through the healer's hands into the etheric field as well as through the chakras of the patient, for the field and the chakras are always tied together.

Almost all healing techniques use the hands to some degree. Whether or not one consciously visualizes the relationship between the heart chakra and the small centers in the palms of the hand, there is a degree of reciprocity between the two. So when the centers in the hands are activated in healing, thereby becoming more sensitized and open, the heart chakra is also stimulated. As for the other chakras, they can be involved in specific cases. But in contrast with some other healers, I do not advocate working directly on the chakras, except that it is always helpful to send energy to the solar plexus, and since the heart chakra is the center of higher energies and of integration, it too is a focus for healing.

The Practice of Visualization

When people have been chronically ill for a long time, they often form a clear and definite mental image of their condition, especially when the diagnosis has made them apprehensive. They picture themselves as sick and deteriorating. Therefore if, after some treatments, patients experience a reduction in their anxiety and also feel more energetic, a next step would be to help them work towards a different mental picture or image of themselves.

At this point it is often useful to ask patients to visualize themselves as getting stronger and more energetic every day. By so doing, their minds can slowly develop and strengthen the idea that they can bring about change in themselves. Such a new self-image obviously cannot be created overnight; it takes time and a consistent effort, for a negative self-image is one of the most difficult attitudes for a patient to change.

Nevertheless, visualization techniques have been used very successfully with patients suffering from cancer, for by this means they are able to mobilize their own energies to combat the disease. When a major disease strikes, it can have a very damaging effect, because when there seems to be little improvement, the patient may begin to despair that anything can be done. This creates a feeling of helplessness and hopelessness which saps normal self-confidence.

The same reaction can result from an emotionally traumatic event, for the anxiety and depression which follow can also lead to a loss of self-confidence. This situation is difficult to work with, because the individual is often unaware of the degree to which a negative self-image has become entrenched. To be of assistance in such a case, it is important not only to perceive the presence of such a negative self-image, but also to be able to communicate this knowledge to the sufferer. One must try to instill a new sense of self-confidence in patients by always thinking of them as being able to function. They must learn to visualize themselves in a way that is directly opposite to the negative self-image they have been developing for so many years. If they have been thinking of themselves as weak, they must see themselves as strong; if sick, as perfectly well.

This exercise, regularly practiced, helps the healing process a great deal. The most important contribution that patients can make toward their own healing is to think of themselves — to visualize themselves — as able to achieve something every day. Even when one feels sick and weak, such positive visualization gives one mental energy, and breaks the negative pattern of saying, "I am too sick; I can't make the effort." A positive self-image helps to overcome the pattern of accepting illness as inevitable.

Visualization actually takes place at the mental level, but since mind and emotions always work together, the practice stimulates and energizes the brow chakra. This in turn helps to coordinate the chakra system, thereby integrating the various levels within the patient which may have been fragmented by the disease process. It puts the person in alignment, because the mind focuses the emotions and does not allow them to get out of control.

But perhaps one of the most positive consequences of visualization is that it gives patients a sense of hope that they can make progress, and a strengthened confidence that they are in charge of their own lives once again. In my healing work, I have found that negative mental images are an even greater block to healing than emotional patterns. Therefore, by encouraging the use of a visualization exercise which pictures action of a new and different kind, the patient's own resources can be mobilized to aid the healing process.

Effects of Healing on the Aura

The effects of healing upon the patient's aura can be quite dramatic. First, the influx of emotional energy causes the aura to expand. When this happens, it starts up the process of eliminating some of the disturbances and blockages in the aura, and thus reduces anxiety. This is one of the most powerful effects of the healing. Anxiety produces frightening mental images. But if imagery is used together with the healing, there will be a simultaneous effect: the immune system will be strengthened through the influx of etheric energy, and as the frightening images dissipate, the aura will slowly regain its integration and recover its health.

In the work I have been doing with nurse-healers these past years, I have found that the practice of healing can affect the healer as well as the patient. The practice of centering, and of consciously opening oneself to higher energies, expands and clarifies the aura. I shall have more to say about this in the chapter on meditation and self-transformation, but I cannot leave the subject of healing without commenting that the nurse practitioners who have been opening themselves to these energies, in an effort to help those who are ill, have found that the practice has begun to change them as well, in subtle but meaningful ways.

IX
Changing Emotional Patterns

One of the greatest mysteries about human beings is their ability to make changes in their lives, to take a wholly new direction. Dramatic transformations of this kind usually take place when life calls forth the utmost effort, and their success depends upon a real confidence in one's ability to succeed. In such cases, the motivation for change usually stems from a condition — whether caused by illness or some other factor — which can no longer be ignored or accepted. It is when we become aware of the necessity for a new direction in our lives, and determine to find it, that change becomes possible.

For many of us, the principal obstacle to change lies in the fact that our emotional habits are so much a part of our nature that we are not aware of them. We may feel their unhappy effects for many years before we realize that we can do something about them.

When we have come to recognize that there are problems within ourselves, the first step is to be willing to admit that these problems are at least partly of our own making, and that if we want to resolve them we ourselves must be willing to change. There are a lot of people who say, "I am what I am and I cannot change." Such people become so set in a habitual emotional pattern that there seems to be very little possibility for a real alteration in their lives. They would rather cling to their illnesses — which give them a kind of security — than let them go.

On the other hand, many people are dissatisfied with themselves and really want to be different, yet they feel unable to help themselves. When our emotional patterns have become established because circumstances have driven us, we may feel that we have no control over our emotional responses even though they make us very unhappy. The results of such a negative attitude can be plainly seen in case #17, which is an example of what can happen when emotional patterns become so ingrained that they dominate us.

But we do not need to be the victims of our own feelings. When we grow more aware of our emotional habits, we begin to understand that these habits are largely self-created. Circumstances may be beyond our control, but our response to them need never be. We do not have to give in to them. There is a strength within us which is still more powerful, and we can release it within us when we are determined to change our future.

Motivation is the first requirement. The very ill often succeed, because those who are desperate are willing to do anything to achieve relief. Thus for some people motivation arises out of the need to overcome illness, but for others the spur for action may arise out of affectionate concern for someone else, or the aspiration to be more peaceful and harmonious within themselves. In any case, recognition of the need to break negative emotional patterns is a basic requirement.

In an effort to bring about personal change, religious groups such as Christian and Zen monastic orders exercise strict discipline upon their members. I once had a strong and healthy young man come to me. He had been brought up a Catholic in a conventional American household and had gone to an ordinary public school, where he had become a good football player and all-around athlete. He was not particularly religious, and seemed a typical American boy. Although he had not had any previous contact with the East, it happened that circumstances took him to India, and while there he visited Dharmasala, the seat of the Dalai Lama and the center of Tibetan Buddhism. He was tremendously impressed both with the Buddhist teaching and the way of life it engendered, and then and there he decided he wanted to become a monk.

For two years this young American underwent the most rigorous training of a kind totally foreign to his cultural or religious background. Tibetan monastic practice, which is aimed at ridding oneself of the ego, includes the chanting of mantrams, as well as sitting motionless in meditation for long periods of time. After two years of this stringent practice, he was initiated and became a monk. Such an achievement required real determination, self-management, and the ability to accept discipline. He has since fulfilled a number of assignments in Europe and the West; setting aside his own ego, he has put himself at the service of Tibetan Buddhism. This is a remarkable achievement for an independent and individualistic young American.

I cite this man as an example of one who obviously determined to change his life, and was willing to submit himself to the most rigorous discipline in order to achieve his goal. He also changed his emotional nature as a result of training himself to let go of the ego. His may be an extreme case, but it illustrates the point I am trying to make: in order to change, one must be completely whole-hearted in the effort, and be willing to give up all one's former habits of thought and behavior. Though it may not be necessary for most people to alter their way of life as dramatically as this young man did, there must be a willingness to do so.

The effort to break emotional patterns cannot be hesitant or sporadic; it must be constant. When you believe that the need for change is important, this need will come first. It is not too different from the kind of training to which athletes are willing and eager to subject themselves in order to achieve excellence in sports, or the self-discipline which is required to rid yourself of a bad habit such as smoking. If you skip several days, or fall back into old habits, the effort will be wasted. The determination for self-change must override other interests and desires.

For these reasons, the most important factors in the process of change are motivation, self-confidence and consistency. When these are all strong, the practice of a disciplined effort can be not only acceptable but even pleasurable, for it becomes integrated into daily life as an ordering or stabilizing principle.

The Need for Discipline

The acceptance of discipline follows naturally when you have made up your mind that it is essential to your purpose. In some ways, the discipline imposed by an accepted practice such as Zen training is the easiest to follow, because the rules have already been set for you. But this kind of training is not for everyone, and many people find it too restrictive. Self-imposed discipline has the advantage that it can be tailored to your needs, but it demands the same degree of structure in daily life; moreover, you have to create this structure yourself, which can be difficult to do. But here again, the discipline is not too different from that required by the personal fitness programs which are so popular today, for these also demand constant attention to one's daily schedule.

Perhaps one of the reasons why athletes are so admired is because they are totally dedicated to their art. I believe that many of the difficulties which young people experience today are due to the absence of purpose in their lives; they drift, not knowing what they want to do or be. For them, the lack of guidance is disorienting. It is not total freedom that they need, in spite of what is often proclaimed, but rather the opposite movement toward the development of some structure and purpose around which to organize their lives.

Older people often deplore the loss of values and ethics in modern society. I do myself. But every age has it own values, and today the cry is for freedom—freedom from the restrictions of conventional morality, freedom of choice, freedom of action, and above all, freedom to be oneself. Older values, like honesty and authenticity, become all mixed up with the impulse of the moment, which has become the criterion of freedom. So this behavior has an element of idealism, even if the results are far from ideal.

The feeling that one has an absolute right to freedom and its expression is often so powerful that it seems life is not worth living without it. This conviction is behind the former flight of young people in Eastern Europe to the West, for which they were willing to put themselves and their families at risk. We applaud this. But among a large number of young people the passion for freedom becomes tied to their sexuality, which in turn becomes their overriding concern, more important than anything else. They then develop an emotional pattern of dependency upon such stimulus. They do not realize that in their search for freedom they have merely exchanged one form of bondage for another. If I were able to show you the aura of such a person you would see a total disjuncture between the top, which would be full of idealism, and the bottom, which would be marred by compulsive behavior.

A Sense of Purpose

Everyone needs freedom to develop his or her potentials, but a sense of purpose is also needed, for this alone provides the grounding which can establish a feeling of self-worth. All the examples in Chapter VI had such a sense of purpose, even if it led them in very different directions. When the confidence that one can make something worthwhile of life is lacking, many people take to alcohol or drugs, and that habit is probably the very worst pattern they could fall into.

It is common knowledge today that drug addiction is very difficult to cure, because the addict himself must have a strong motivation to change. But when the desire to achieve some purpose in life provides such motivation, anything is possible. I once knew a man who had been a drug addict for many years, during the course of which he had even spent some years in prison. In spite of all his physical and psychological problems, he was an intelligent man who retained his interest in new ideas, and because of this he happened to attend one of my husband's lectures on integrative education. He was so struck by the possibilities which seemed to open up before him that he immediately decided he was going to enlist himself in this work.

I suppose one might call this sudden development of purpose a kind of conversion—in some ways similar to that of the young Tibetan monk. All at once, this addicted man realized that there was a whole world of ideas which he wanted to enter, and that he would never be able to do so if he remained on drugs. Despite his excellent mind, this was more than a purely rational decision. He had a sudden insight into a richer domain of experience, and all at once life had new meaning for him.

This man's desire to work with my husband in the Center for Integrative Education was so powerful that he did something which medical practitioners regard as almost impossible: he locked himself up for three days and nights and detoxified himself without help — an extremely difficult and painful thing to do. He emerged cured in the sense that he never took drugs again, but of course his nervous system had been so damaged that his health was never really normal. Nevertheless he achieved his object, and worked for the Center for several years. This is an example of what a human being can accomplish when the power of the will is mobilized by commitment to a goal.

The transformative power of such self-commitment comes from a level within us which lies beyond thought and feeling. One cannot reason a person into the need for change; the conviction has to be self-generated. But when this inner conviction is born in us, it is a never-ending source of strength. This means that there is something in all of us, some center of power and purpose which we can draw on in time of need. I have called this center the timeless self because it is always there for us, if only we will make the effort to reach it.

Self-Awareness

In order to effect change, the first necessity is to watch ourselves, most of all at the moment when we feel strongly about something — and these surges of emotion can often be triggered by a relatively unimportant event. It is only by such watchfulness that we can become aware of the strength of our feelings and recognize their object, which often does not warrant so great a response as we have been making. This recognition makes it possible for us to see the situation in perspective, to laugh at ourselves and say, "Now I am going to let go, to disassociate myself from my feeling and see what its consequences are."

The first thing to perceive is that we can only become aware of an emotion right at the moment that we are feeling it. The reason is that when feelings are habitual they become embedded in us — tied to everything we feel and do — and therefore go unnoticed. They are as much a part of ourselves as a hand or a foot — about which we never think. Like #11's orange plume, we become so habituated to the emotional patterns we have built up that we are unaware of their presence until something calls them to our attention.

However, once we have become aware of a feeling such as anger or resentment, and recognized its presence in us, we can take the next step, which is to be still within ourselves. We should not feel guilt for the anger, or blame ourselves, because judgments of this kind only set up another reaction and lead to all sorts of negative complications. The important thing is just to be aware of the feeling, and then to be still for a moment. Within this stillness the automatic action of our patterned emotional response temporarily ceases. Stillness is a state which is free from past associations, and therefore it offers the possibility of something new and different.

There are many people today who really long for the ability to transform themselves. Even if they are not able to define the nature of their aspiration, it is really a kind of spiritual quest. They are stirred by self-discontent; they aspire to be better without knowing just how to embark on their search for spiritual values.

To such people, I suggest that all of us have our own talents, and if we can become aware of what they are we should try to foster them. Such talents are not necessarily creative gifts; they may lie in the field of human relations. Many people today are overwhelmed by the magnitude of the world's problems, and frustrated because they believe there is nothing they can contribute. They feel isolated — locked up in their own lives.

The positive way to deal with this frustration is to find something to do for someone else. It need not be anything earth-shaking — just a simple offer of friendship and good will. There is all too little of this today. But if even this seems too difficult, then extend your care to an animal, like a cat or dog. The important thing is to become confident that you can feel concern and affection, and then express your feeling through some specific action. This makes a break in the pattern of emotional isolation.

Habit Patterns

In some of the aura pictures you will have seen evidence that certain memories or ideas or associations have such a strong emotional component that they become a part of a person's inner life, and appear in the aura as semi-permanent symbols. I usually call these emotional structures, to distinguish them from the more temporary patterns like the small whirls and vortices which result from irritation, worry, disappointment, and so on. These deep-seated structures may result from an experience which was painful, but they can also come from an association which was so inspiring that it remains fresh and vivid for a long time. The trees in the aura of case #11 came to symbolize peace as well as deep protective feelings for nature, while the symbolic forms in case #12 represent a past association whose memory continued to sustain and uplift that woman all her life. In contrast, the faces that appear in #8 and #14 symbolize an abiding concern for people and their well-being.

I have been asked why some experiences become incorporated in the aura in such symbolic forms, while others are not. Our experience is of course also embodied in the colors of the aura, which change quite slowly. I think the symbols are related to a person's fundamental way of thinking and seeing the world. For example, #7 is a man who felt uncomfortable in a disorganized environment, and who always tried to bring order into his surroundings. Case #13 was also tremendously concerned with order, but in him it was a much more abstract, intellectual interest.

Habit patterns begin very early in life. From my observation of people of different ages, I have come to the conclusion that their difficulties often stem from a lack of self-confidence. This tendency develops early in childhood. It may come from constant parental criticism or from a child's feeling of being somehow different from other children. However engendered, it can all too easily develop into a sense of uncertainty. A basic lack of self-confidence should not be confused with shyness, which is common in young children because they are as yet unable to relate to people outside of their family. A lack of self-confidence, in contrast, shows up in relationships within the family as well as with strangers.

Roots of Self-Confidence

It is sometimes hard for us to realize how important early childhood relationships are. A sense of insecurity often grows out of a child's inability to understand the reasons behind his parents' actions. It is naturally important to correct children's behavior, but on the other hand, one should not expect perfection. Parents should never expose a child to constant criticism without an equal or greater amount of encouragement. Unfortunately, many children have a basic lack of self-confidence because their parents never helped them to realize that they were able to do some things very well.

If children have physical disabilities which they must learn to live with, it is particularly important for them to realize that emotional and mental capacities are just as important as a good physical body. They must learn to rely on the strengths they have. The development of self-confidence takes root early and can sustain a person throughout life. Unlike egotism, which constantly needs to be fed, self-confidence gives people the conviction that they have the strength and capacity to accomplish certain things and to achieve their goals in life.

Lack of self-confidence is, I think, a basic human problem. It is a major cause of chronic depression, which is very damaging and difficult to live with, as well as all too common in our present-day culture. It can also develop into a pattern of anxiety, for when we are insecure in our relationships with others we tend to worry constantly about how they will respond to us. Without self-confidence, we never believe that what we have accomplished is really any good, no matter what people may say. Anxiety is a very corrosive emotion, for it eats away our ambition, and makes us doubt our own judgment.

Handling Anger

There was a time when some therapists advocated that feelings should always be openly expressed: if you felt anger you should let it out. I would handle anger quite differently. When you feel the anger rising, I agree that you should say, "I am angry," for it is extremely important to recognize the feeling which is welling up in you, and not repress it. All too often, people rationalize their anger, or deny it, or give it another name, or say it is the fault of someone else or of something that happened. In other words, they will not take the responsibility for their anger. If you say, "I have a right to be angry because you have hurt me," then there is nothing to stop your anger's flow of energy. You are reinforcing it by giving it the seal of your approval.

So, if you are angry, you should never deny it, but it is important to say to yourself, "I admit that *at this moment* I am angry." There are times when we can't help being angry, and then it is important to be honest about it. But if you add the words, "at this moment," you are also saying that you are going to work it out, get rid of it. In other words, "I'm angry, but I'm not going to give in to it or let it dominate me." Such a statement is a kind of signal to ourselves that we refuse anger as a permanent condition. It helps to prevent the development of a sense of suppressed resentment which can persist weeks and even months and years, growing into an implacable dislike. If you admit to yourself that you flared up and became angry, you will not unconsciously incorporate it as part of yourself. On the other hand, you should not pay too much attention to it, brood over it or feel guilty, because then you only reenact your anger and thereby reinforce it.

When a pattern of suppressed anger has built up over the years it turns into resentment, which is one of the most difficult of emotional states to overcome. Anger flares up suddenly, and unless it becomes habitual one can get rid of it fairly quickly. Resentment, on the other hand, is the result of anger which has been suppressed, usually because a person was not in a position to let it out. It is therefore often combined with a feeling of helplessness and frustration, and as a result it can go on smoldering for years, eating away at one's self-esteem and poisoning personal relationships. It is much more subtle than anger and much harder to get rid of, because it can lie hidden within us for such a long time.

Habits of anxiety and resentment may start early in life. If we feel that we have been unfairly treated, either by our parents or by some friend, it is natural to feel angry and resentful at the moment. It is when such resentment builds over months and even years that it becomes so damaging. We begin to perceive other people as exhibiting some of the same characteristics we have resented, and then it can poison all our relationships.

Breaking Negative Patterns

I once knew a successful business woman who came to me so unhappy in her work that she thought she ought to resign. Although her position in the company was important and responsible, she so detested the man she had to work with that her satisfaction in her career was completely spoiled. She felt that his brusqueness and discourtesy were the result of an implacable dislike which he was directing at her, thereby destroying her self-confidence.

My advice to her was that she should reverse roles with this man. Instead of seeing herself as the victim of his negative emotions, she should make a positive effort to send him thoughts of sympathy and compassion—which he must surely need if he was so disagreeable. The resulting change in her own feelings made her reach out to him much more easily, and as a consequence the barriers between them fell, and he confided to her all the troubles which had made him so difficult. Since these problems had nothing to do with her personally, she understood their relationship quite differently, and this put it on a wholly new footing.

Incidents of this kind show to what degree resentment can cloud our perception of others, and hamper our ability to make clear, impersonal judgments about our relationships. In order to break out of such a destructive pattern, we have to become aware of what the feeling of resentment or lack of self-confidence is based on. When we realize that we are succumbing to the same kind of strong negative reaction we have felt repeatedly, we should stop, take a deep breath, and say lightly to ourselves, "Hey, here I am doing the same old thing over again." Then we should deliberately change the pattern of our thinking by visualizing some pleasant scene or memory. This will shift the focus of our attention and break the cycle of automatic reaction.

Depression is another chronic emotional pattern. Akin to anxiety, it is difficult to handle because it not only drains the body's energy but also slows energy intake to such a degree that effort is almost impossible, and one becomes very lethargic. This is why physical movement is such an important part of therapy. Walking is good exercise, and it can energize a person enough to change his or her mood. I often recommend folk dancing, because rhythmic movement done to music is in itself harmonizing, and because the companionship of the other dancers stimulates a helpful human interaction. While dancing a person is performing an ordered movement in a group of people who are all intent on the same thing, and who are therefore friendly and accepting. The dancing itself is invigorating, and the fact that one is able to do it successfully conveys a sense of accomplishment.

The Place of Idealism

If we had something in our culture that reinforced the spiritual dimension which I have defined as the source of the true self in each of us, we would be encouraged to try to find and experience that self for ourselves. We could accept its reality as part of the human potential—

an ideal which is possible to actualize in our own lives. Idealism has unfortunately become downgraded in our culture. The implication is that it is not realistic, that it has no rational basis, that it is impractical, that it is at variance with life experience, and so on. But idealism and practicality are far from being incompatible. Over history, the people who have changed the world were idealists who had their feet on the ground and knew how to accomplish their goals.

I have said that human beings need goals to create motivation, and goals are usually based on an ideal of excellence. Motivation, in turn, arises out of confidence in oneself — a feeling of self-worth. Many people do not seem to perceive the great difference between self-confidence and egotism. Self-worth generates the confidence that you can overcome your difficulties and limitations, and this makes your energies flow outward freely. In fact, a strong sense of self is an essential element in all creative action.

Those who are self-centered turn their energies toward their bodies. This blocks their normal ability to be sensitive to others. They become overly interested in how they feel, and this becomes a dominant factor in their lives and may lead to sickness and depression.

In contrast, reformers like our case #11 have a strong sense of self, but at the same time they are idealists. These are the world's shakers and movers. Reformers may be mistaken or even bigoted, but their motivation is fundamentally the good of others. They feel very strongly that they know what should be done, and how to do it, and the power of their conviction mobilizes many around them. It is only when their self-confidence swells into self-righteousness and their zeal turns to fanaticism that they become dangerous, for then they cannot tolerate dissent. (This is the condition #11 recognized as incipient in his own orange plume, which he then determined to get rid of.)

Altruism

There is a point of view that everything you do stems basically from self-interest, and that if you try to be helpful to someone else it is only because you get satisfaction from the effort. Of course you get satisfaction, but that is not the reason you do it. Others suggest that you do good works in life in order to be rewarded for them in an afterlife, instead of simply because they are needed. Chogyam Trungpa, a Tibetan lama, had a good expression for this attitude. He called it spiritual materialism, which means giving so that you can get some reward — a kind of spiritual quid pro quo. But all the religions teach that simply offering your help because someone needs it is the basis of right action. Unfortunately, in our educational system today, the acceptance of altruism as a ruling principle in life has all but disappeared.

Many people, however, are very troubled about our world's problems. They wish with all their hearts that they could do something positive to help, but mistrust their own capabilities. The important thing to realize is that we can all make some contribution according to our own abilities. In these times of stress we can help by trying not to react to the stress around us. Two or three times a day center yourself and be a center of peace, sending out thoughts of peace. This action has definite positive effects. It supports our altruistic aspiration to serve humanity, and at the same time develops our closer relationship with the upper reaches of our consciousness and with what I have called the timeless self.

I never suggest that people should not have a satisfying personal life. The personal gains added importance, however, when we become aware of its universal background. It is in terms of the whole of human life that our own experience takes on meaning and proves its value. When the bonds of narrow self-interest are broken by the force of altruism, our affection and good will are released to discharge their energy freely into the larger world of human relationships. This benefits everyone.

X
Meditation and the Growth of Intuition

In previous chapters I have indicated some of the basic attitudes and efforts that are needed in order to effect changes in emotional patterns. Now I want to carry this a step further, and talk about self-transformation in a deeper sense.

The desire to learn, to grow, to transcend our limitations, is basic in all of us. We study, take degrees, train ourselves in different skills in order to improve our minds; we exercise, watch our diets, play games in order to improve our physical health. I have tried to show that we can also cultivate and improve our emotions when we find it is important for us to do so. Beyond this, many of us aspire to become more caring and more altruistic — to rid ourselves of narrow attitudes and selfish motives. Having become convinced that there is a spiritual reality that is deeper, more enduring, more joyful, more compassionate, more unitive than anything else we can experience in life, we want to align ourselves with that reality. To do so, we know instinctively that we must try to escape the bondage of the personal ego.

These are some of the reasons why people undertake Zen training, practice yoga or Sufi dancing or study Tibetan Buddhism. All of these methods can help us towards the goal of self-transformation; all incorporate some form of meditation or mental discipline in order to open the student to the possibilities of a different kind of awareness. Meditation is often advocated as a relaxation technique or a method of reducing stress, and it can be very helpful in these ways. But it has much deeper aspects. Its greatest potential benefit lies in the fact that it offers the possibility of access to dimensions of consciousness which lie beyond the personal self.

Meditation may be said to have a twofold purpose. It is a way of relating to the deeper aspects of one's own nature, but it is not only that. It is also a way of relating oneself to a much greater reality which we can think of under different guises: as the unity underlying nature, or the spiritual dimension, or God, or the Divine Milieu. Thus meditation is far from being merely a withdrawal into an inward passive state (as some have asserted). It is a dynamic experience of the identity of the inner self with the whole of things—whose compass is so great as to be, in fact, limitless.

Such an experience can have reciprocal effects. Our need for direction leads us to meditate, and the practice in turn helps to clarify our sense of purpose. This is so because inner quiet gives that purpose a chance to emerge—an achievement which is impossible when we are caught up in the turmoil and conflict which are so much a part of daily life.

Shift of Focus

I have said before that the emergence of purpose arises from that point of consciousness within each of us which is the true or spiritual self— our source of peace and wholeness. Identifying with this timeless self gives us the power of control over our feelings and our actions. It is the source of intuition, of creativity, and of the strength to take the direction of our lives into our own hands. When this power is released within us, it can give us guidance no matter how difficult the circumstances.

Once we become aware of this deeper, more timeless aspect of ourselves we can shift our focus whenever we have a problem, and see it from a larger perspective. The sense of "I" can change with such shifts in focus—away from identification with the circumstances we feel caught in to the freedom of a more universal, less time-bound order. A more open perspective always offers us the possibility of movement and change, because it transcends the purely personal element in our feelings—and it is this which often distorts our relationships with others.

Such a shift of focus also makes us take notice of what is going on in our minds and emotions. We become aware of the level of consciousness at which we are operating at any particular moment, and are able to reestablish our focus where we wish it to be. In this process of developing self-awareness, meditation is useful because it is one of the ways by which we can find the point at which the "I" is focused.

In discussing emotional patterns, I stressed the fact that anxiety is destructive because it makes us feel incapable of coping with the situations that confront us. The reason is that it temporarily blocks the inflow of the higher energies whose source lies within the dimension of wholeness. When our inner connection with the self is blocked, we begin to doubt our self-worth, our confidence is undermined, and we are vulnerable to depression. Even when some degree of inner peace has been achieved, the problem for many people is how to establish such a durable relationship with their fundamental wholeness that it persists in the face of the stresses of daily life. I believe that meditation is one of the most successful means to this achievement.

Fear of Self-Delusion

Unfortunately, many people hesitate to undertake the practice of meditation because they are afraid of being self-deluded. So many of our traditional values have been discarded as irrelevant to the contemporary world that we have the habit of questioning every claim. But there is a big difference between being skeptical in the sense that the Buddha advocated—taking nothing on hearsay, thinking things through for oneself—and the canker of self-doubt, which undermines every value, including the value of our own achievements.

Since it is impossible to prove that anything is absolutely right and true, the fear of being deluded destroys the ability to commit oneself to anything which cannot be measured or demonstrated. But we all know that none of the really important things can be measured, or their value "proved," since they have to do with intangibles.

It is certainly possible to be self-deluded in meditation, just as in anything else. But should this fact prevent us from meditating? If we were afraid that all knowledge might be false we would be doubtful about the usefulness of studying anything. In any event, there is no great danger of self-deception in meditation, because it is not a method of introspection or self-observation, in which one can easily substitute wish for reality. We meditate without expectations of success or failure, concentrating on reaching our own center of peace without trying to define or describe its qualities. This can lead to an experience that is real.

My recommendation, therefore, is that we take the possibility of our access to spiritual reality as a hypothesis which may or may not be true, but which is worth trying out. Then we can experiment and see for ourselves whether this hypothesis stands up in experience. Many people begin to meditate without really believing in it. They are willing to take a chance, even though they are not sure what the results will be. I find this attitude very natural. I also accept the fact that meditation is not for everyone; some preparation is needed, if only acceptance of the fact that the time has come to achieve some inner space and peace. Under such circumstances, one could say to a doubter: Try it, and see for yourself.

I always hope that people will approach meditation as something that can be really enjoyable, even fun, rather than as a solemn task we undertake as a kind of duty to ourselves. It can truly refresh us — give us new energy when we are tired, calm and balance us when we are upset, help us let go of our problems, restore our perspective and sense of proportion. In daily life, our auras are constantly exchanging energies with others, and our attention is usually engaged with what is going on around us. The result is that our focus is outside ourselves. In meditation we intentionally shift that focus within the heart center, thereby creating a concentric flow of energy which is just the opposite of the scattering or diffusing tendency that so much of our daily activity demands.

Stimulating Higher Energies

This is why the practice of meditation not only gives us a feeling of peace, but also energizes us. The experience speeds up the activity of the heart chakra, and this slowly begins to affect the connection with the other higher centers. When this occurs, it opens us to influences from a higher dimension and establishes an emotional pattern which is integrative, in contrast to the conflicting patterns which pull us in different directions during the day. Thus it produces a state of wholeness and inner serenity which can stand us well in times of stress.

In the aura, there are usually many momentary emotional conditions that block the expansion of consciousness. When meditation includes not only a withdrawal into one's center but also a deliberate effort to send peace and love outward into the world, the expansion of the aura which results works directly to break up the scars of traumatic events. The results show in the aura as a lightening of the colors, greater clarity, and a general feeling of harmony, balance and integration. These are subtle differences, but they can perhaps be traced in auras #13, #14 and #18, all of whom were long-term meditators, and also in #7, where meditation had been practiced for a somewhat shorter period.

Meditation stimulates the higher energies, and their release within us changes our perspective radically. The awareness it engenders helps us to see people in a new light, so that we begin to ask ourselves how we affect them, instead of the other way around. We often raise barriers between ourselves and others, but when we try regularly to feel love we lower our defenses and become much more open. In this way we begin to gain a new consciousness of the significance of our interpersonal relations. As we become more sensitive to others, we grow in the ability to interact with them in positive ways.

Meditation Techniques

When we have committed ourselves to finding peace within ourselves, and decided that meditation is a gateway to this peace, then the specific technique we use is not really so important. Some methods suggest reading a passage from the scriptures or chanting mantrams, all of which quiet the mind. Zen and other Buddhist forms of meditation such as Satipatthana stress walking while concentrating on the breath. Rhythmic breathing is certainly important.

Whatever the method, there are certain basic requirements. The first is to relax and become aware that you can experience a sense of stillness within yourself. Therefore it is helpful to breathe in and out deeply several times and relax your shoulders, and then focus in the region of the heart chakra. I always recommend that beginners practice only for a very short time — three to five minutes. The length of time one meditates is not important, so long as the experience is real. People often try to do too much too soon, and therefore become discouraged. Finding that they are unable to still the mind for more than a few minutes at a time, they go on because they think they are obliged to, and so become bored and restless.

For the first three or four months of practice, the main effort should be to find a point of stillness within yourself. Once that has been established, you will slowly get used to meditating, and learn to like it. When I say that, I am also saying that there is an emotional component in meditation. This is true, but the effort to reach a state of stillness transcends ordinary feelings of pleasure and pain, or like and dislike.

At the beginning there may be some ambivalence: you may think you are quiet and at the same time be conscious of a background which is full of distraction. So you will be aware of two things at the same time: your inner peace, and your chattering mind. You can accept this situation without having it distract you from the recognition that at some level you have experienced a real sense of quietude. As you persist, you will reach a deeper level of this stillness, and then you will begin to experience a sense of expansion, a feeling of unity with the universe.

Little by little, as you continue the practice, the stillness will deepen and the mind's chatter will be quieted. Even though your thoughts may intervene and you may be aware of the distraction, you will be able to remain focused within the stillness. The best analogy to this experience I can think of is flying in a plane and breaking through the clouds to the clear blue of the sky beyond.

Meditation in the Heart

I have stressed the importance of focusing in the region of the heart, which I call centering, because the heart is the seat of spiritual as well as physical life. We may ordinarily think that focusing implies a narrowing of attention or awareness, but the opposite is true when we center. The heart chakra is capable of almost unlimited expansion; an analogy might be the circle whose center is everywhere and whose circumference is nowhere. So focused, we experience a sense of unity with nature and with the universe as a whole. This stretches the aura and breaks down restrictive patterns, and the feeling of unity can sharpen, giving a new dimension to all our relationships.

When people are uncertain about their ability to meditate, I usually give them a visualization exercise to help them get started. For example, I suggest that you first withdraw your energies into the heart, and associate this with a feeling of unity with the timeless self. This inner self should be visualized as a light within your heart, within which you consciously withdraw. Feel a sense of peace, and think of yourself as one with the light. Then, if you have a painful memory that bothers you, recall it and deliberately visualize it as being slightly detached from and in front of you. You should try to see it as being outside yourself. Then visualize rays of light shining out from the center of light within your heart, pouring right through that painful memory until it is dissolved.

Many people have found this exercise has given them a wonderful sense of freedom from their anxieties. Moreover, if you want to help someone who is ill or in distress, it is effective to visualize the person surrounded by this light within the heart, and then reach out to him or her on that level.

Detachment

I have said that when we experience the sense of peace within ourselves our perspective on the world and on our relationships begins to change. One of the differences is a growth of detachment. There seems to be a great deal of misunderstanding about the meaning of this word, which people mistakenly confuse with the kind of cold impersonality that stands aloof from the pains and troubles of others. Detachment does not mean that we cease to feel for others or to sympathize with their suffering. It does mean that we do not personally involve ourselves in their problems on an emotional level — which actually can prevent us from being of much service to them. Nurses know from experience that they cannot help a patient who is in pain unless they are able to maintain their own inner strength and serenity.

When you center yourself in meditation you are consciously experiencing wholeness, your undivided unity with everything that exists. You see yourself, as well as the people with whom you have relationships, as part of that immense wholeness. It is in this sense that we interact with one another most authentically. On the personal level we are always separated from each other by the barriers of the ego, but these barriers do not exist at that deeper level. When we are able to detach ourselves from personal interest, we can reach out to people in a much more enduring way.

Projecting Love

Meditation assists in this process because it brings down energy from a more universal dimension. If we want to develop this potential and use it fully we should try to feel love every day, and project it to anyone who we feel might need it. This is important for many reasons. Too often we think that love is only fulfilling if it is reciprocated, and when this synchronism between people does not take place the result is a lot of pain. If our love is personal it can be unconsciously demanding, and this aggravates our emotional problems.

In meditation, however, we experience a different kind of love, an outflow or giving of the self that is undemanding and requires no return. When we are able to send out love unreservedly, without doubt or fear of loss or thought of self, then that energy will reach others at a higher level, where they can use it to mobilize their own inner powers, and help them to resolve their problems. This is what I mean by detachment.

When you center yourself in meditation you are consciously experiencing a sense of unity on this deeper level. You feel yourself, as well as the people with whom you have relationships, as part of a greater whole. You thus begin to realize, as a matter of experience, that the same potential for wholeness and peace exists in everyone, and in sending thoughts of love to others, you are trying to reach them at that deeper level. In so doing, you open yourself to the much greater and more potent energies of a higher dimension. Therefore, if you want to develop this potential and use it to the fullest, you should try regularly to project as much love as possible. As the Dalai Lama has said, if we would all feel peace and compassion, there would be an end to war and violence. In times like these, when the world is shaken by doubt and anxiety, we can help to lighten the atmosphere of the whole Earth by sending out the energies of peace and love.

Intuition

In various contexts, I have indicated that there is an aspect of consciousness within us which is called the intuition—the kind of immediate understanding which reaches beyond the usual processes of the mind and gives direct insight. This power is not limited to a few geniuses, but resides as a potentiality within all of us. As a matter of fact, many of us do experience this level of consciousness at some moment in our lives. At times when everything seems to go wrong, if we become still for a moment, there can arise out of that stillness a conviction of the right course for us to take. In the moment of crisis we are suddenly filled with strength; we know we can keep calm. It is the intuition which tells us without words what we should do.

The sense of unity which is realized in meditation opens us up this intuitive capacity, which is related to the timeless self. Intuition or insight means seeing into the heart of things. It gives us a momentary opening into a higher dimension of direct understanding, or clear seeing, which leaps over the limitations of our usual thinking processes in a flash of unitive perception.

Thus if we are really searching for the right course to take—for the secret of right action, as the Buddhists say—and can be still within ourselves, the intuition may open. Then we can get an insight into the direction we should go, and into a plan of action—a plan which is not entirely dependent on the facts we have to work with, for these may be inadequate for our purpose.

Intuition comes from a far deeper dimension of consciousness than ordinary thinking. It can illuminate our search for understanding by bringing about a new synthesis. Numerous scientists have testified to their experience of such a flash of intuition, which suddenly brought bits of knowledge together in an unforeseen relationship. Thus intuition always raises us to a new level of meaning, an expanded vision of reality. It can operate on many levels, but since it is an insight into the unity underlying the phenomena of life, its results persist and deepen through time.

There are different degrees of intuition, and these are not necessarily all connected with large impersonal issues. Intuitions can come to quite simple people, for they do not throw up the barriers of the critical mind to insights from within. Intuition always confers an unshakable sense of certainty and authenticity; we do not hesitate to accept it and act upon it. When we have a flash of intuition, there is for that moment an integration of the different dimensions of consciousness within us, and the result is a conviction that we have found the truth of the problem that confronts us.

The reason such intuitions do not occur more frequently is that our thoughts are usually disordered. When our minds are distracted in many different directions, we run into the danger that threatens our age: knowing everything and understanding nothing. Intuition does not work unless the mind offers it a clear avenue of access, for the mind is the instrument for translating insights into action. When the mind is transparent to spiritual insight, the result is *prajna*, as the Buddhists call it, or wisdom. The implication is that every human being has a point of contact with a dimension of consciousness of which truth is an aspect. What meditation can do, therefore, is clear the mind so that the intuition can come through.

Many people would like to be able to develop a technique for unfolding the intuition, so that the experience might occur more frequently. I do not think it possible to plan ahead for an intuitional experience, but certainly the ground can be prepared, and for this one must learn to still the mind and not let noisy thoughts intrude without permission.

The Unitive Experience

The transformation that comes through religious conversion begins at the same level, but it is much more encompassing. As in the case of St. Francis (and many others, such as Mother Teresa in our own times), it may come suddenly, but the whole life has been a preparation for this moment, when all of the energies — not only of body and mind, but of the spirit as well — are fused into a whole. In a flash the clouds dissolve, the barriers fall, and there comes an awakening to spiritual reality which penetrates and transforms every level, right through to the physical body.

But there are smaller openings of insight which fall short of such total conversion, yet give us glimpses into the nature of spiritual reality. When we see a beautiful landscape and feel ourselves to be a part of it, we have a sense of participating in a far greater whole than we have knowledge of. Many of us have the same sense when listening to music. The experience of beauty touches the heart, expanding the boundaries of the self to such a degree that it can truthfully be called a unitive experience — for one loses the feeling of being locked within oneself, or limited to the consciousness of the I.

Meditation is not for all, but it is one of the gateways to this unitive experience. The interesting thing is that our feeling of expansion, which seems to include the whole world, is attained by withdrawing into the stillness within ourselves. Without and within are no longer opposed to one another. This happens because we quiet the turbulence of our emotional and mental life, which usually makes it impossible for us to "listen" to the stillness within. Thus we regain our sense of being part of a universal whole within which nothing is forgotten, no one left out.

When we experience this level of wholeness, we are drawing upon a different kind of energy, and this energy will slowly penetrate the other levels of consciousness. If meditation is habitual, the feeling of unity with the world is never entirely lost; it becomes the background of life. When we become conscious of this level, we are filled with new energies, and this can have a transforming effect. We experience this in different ways through meditation — sometimes as a rush of love and sympathy, sometimes as a clarity of mind, sometimes in visual images or symbols, sometimes as a release of creative imagination, sometimes as the ability to act out our deepest beliefs and convictions.

Integration of All the Levels

The practice of meditation can therefore strengthen the potentialities innate within us. It can give us the ability to remain calm and stable throughout our difficulties. It can become so integrated into our lives that its presence influences everything we say and do. When we reach this stage, meditation is not only a formal practice for which we sit. It becomes a link that we can reestablish through a moment's attention. Thus the higher energies which are awakened can become an active ingredient of daily life.

Thus, slowly, energies of which we have been unaware are released, and become more active in us. When the mind and emotions have learned to be sensitive to the higher dimensions, these energies can be drawn upon as they are needed. As we become more attentive to them they become more real to us — a resource which has many practical uses. Through achieving a sense of unity with the inner, timeless self, we develop the will and the motivation to break old, restrictive patterns and rebuild ourselves — and it is we, ourselves, who have produced this transformation.

If it is our firm intention to live in harmony with the whole of things, this intent cannot be confined to the few minutes a day we spend in meditation. It has to be brought through into every dimension of our consciousness, including the physical. Even when meditation is practiced regularly over a considerable period of time, it does not change us until it begins to permeate our action. But when this happens, our intention becomes a tool to help us handle our difficulties, a weapon to help us defeat our selfish impulses — most especially in the arena of interpersonal relations. When the sense of unity experienced in meditation persists throughout the day, our lives begin to reflect our spiritual aspirations. Our focus, then, is no longer limited to the narrow constraints of the personal self — the ego — for it has expanded into the universal dimension of the self which knows no boundaries.

In this world, everything is connected with everything else. When, in our meditation, we begin to realize that the physical world is essentially one with — an expression of — spiritual reality, we have a deeper appreciation of the significance of human life. This can change us in the most profound sense, because our thoughts, our actions, everything we feel and do, will flow naturally from that understanding.

We do not need to become saints or ascetics in order to begin this process of integration. It requires only a real intent, a serious commitment. Then, no matter how many mistakes we make, the stream of our daily life will be a continuation of our meditation, and our highest ideals will become an integral part of our action and our experience.

This, the integration of the timeless with the personal self, is the goal — not only of the one who meditates but of everyone who searches for the true meaning of human life.

QUEST BOOKS
are published by
The Theosophical Society in America,
Wheaton, Illinois 60189-0270,
a branch of a world organization
dedicated to the promotion of brotherhood and
the encouragement of the study of religion,
philosophy, and science, to the end that man may
better understand himself and his place in
the universe. The Society stands for complete
freedom of individual search and belief.
In the Classics Series well-known
theosophical works are made
available in popular editions.